ASTROLOGY

 a beginner's guide

GRAHAM BOSTON

Hodder & Stoughton
A MEMBER OF THE HODDER HEADLINE GROUP

Acknowledgements

With thanks to Teresa Moorey for giving me the opportunity to write this book, to Fiona Megginson for giving such valuable feedback and to James Hunt for his positivity and encouragement.

The author and publishers would also like to thank W. Foulsham & Co. Ltd for permission to reproduce the Proportional Logarithms Table (Figure 13), previously published in *Raphael's Astronomical Ephemeris of the Planet's Places for 1997*.

Orders: please contact Bookpoint Ltd, 78 Milton Park, Abingdon, Oxon OX14 4TD. Telephone: (44) 01235 827720, Fax: (44) 01235 400454. Lines are open from 9.00–6.00, Monday to Saturday, with a 24 hour message answering service. Email address: orders@bookpoint.co.uk

British Library Cataloguing in Publication Data
A catalogue record for this title is available from The British Library

ISBN 0 340 77485 1

First published 1998
This edition published 2000
Impression number 10 9 8 7 6 5 4 3 2 1
Year   2005 2004 2003 2002 2001 2000 1999

Typeset by Transet Limited, Coventry, England.
Printed in Great Britain for Hodder & Stoughton Educational, a division of Hodder Headline plc, 338 Euston Road, London NW1 3BH by Cox and Wyman Limited, Reading, Berks.

CONTENTS

INTRODUCTION

Imagine you are floating in the vast reaches of outer space. Above you and around you the velvety blackness of infinity is punctuated by showers of stars, scattered like wheat from an invisible hand. The stars form patterns, like the faces that appear and disappear in clouds. First a ram's head, then a bull, then two figures hand in hand, and then a crab. As you turn, more appear, until a ring of twelve symbols forms around you, full of mysterious significance.

You are the Sun and, around you, nine planets circulate. Each emits a sound, like instruments in a cosmic orchestra. As they orbit, you hear different passages, some pleasantly harmonious, others dissonant and clashing. Loud crescendos evoking movement and action give way to soft, reflective tones evoking stillness and contemplation. You are moved by the majesty of it all. Slowly, the music fades and you glide gently down to Earth, your home and your body. It has been a memorable vision.

So how on Earth can there be a link between the planets and a person's character? Scientists say it is impossible, that it flies in the face of accepted beliefs about how the universe works. Perhaps we simply haven't found all the answers yet. The universe may be a good deal more mysterious, even more magical, than we realise. Sometimes it is better to form our own judgements and trust our own experience, than always to listen to those who say something can't be true.

Astrology is a big and exciting subject, far bigger than the scope of this book. It is a journey of discovery that lasts a lifetime, perhaps many lifetimes, and there is always something new waiting to be found. Let's take the first step!

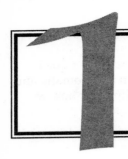

why Learn astrology?

*M*ost people encounter astrology through reading the 'Sun sign' or 'star sign' columns in newspapers or magazines. Whilst they are often fun to read, they bear little relation to 'real' astrology as practised by those who understand the art, even though they are often written by highly skilled, professional astrologers. The premise that the same forecast can apply to one-twelfth of the world's population obviously stretches belief. However, as we shall discover, a person's Sun sign is important, and such columns are often used as a way of bringing broader astrological concepts to the public.

From a person's date, time and place of birth, astrology takes into account not only the Sun sign, but many other factors too, building up a sophisticated picture of the total person.

The aim of this book is to introduce you to a subject that has the potential to enrich your life and reveal the matrix of hidden patterns underlying so-called 'everyday reality'. With the knowledge and the skills you gain, you can master its basic techniques and become fluent in the language of astrology. You will then be able to put astrology to the test in your own life and decide for yourself whether it is simply a matter of self-delusion, or whether it contains truths that give you insight into your own life.

making choices — fate and free will

Some people believe that astrology is incompatible with free will, that events in one's life are predetermined in ways that even the most avid geneticists would not support. Whilst this is a perfectly

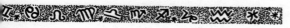

coherent position to hold, most astrologers believe that a horoscope tells us about an individual's *predispositions and preferences*. Just because we have a particular predisposition, for instance a quick temper, it does not mean that we cannot behave in a diplomatic and sensitive manner in the right circumstances. It is up to us how we manifest the potentials symbolised by the horoscope.

Knowing our own horoscope can, in fact, give us more choices, as it enables us to be clearer about who we are and what we can become. We can choose to work with the inherent challenges or weaknesses in our nature and grow towards wholeness as a consequence. Unlike some forms of psychotherapy, which seek to analyse the present mainly in terms of childhood events, astrology can be used as a catalyst for personal development and to reconnect with our *whole* selves.

Although astrologers sometimes make predictions, these are based on astrological *forecasts*. Like a weather forecast, they let us know what kind of 'cosmic weather' is on the horizon, and what kinds of opportunities and challenges we face. We can know when to make hay while the Sun shines, or when to seek shelter from an approaching storm. Equally, we could choose to ignore the Sun and stay indoors, or we could plan a picnic or barbecue for the next downpour. Knowing what influences are likely to occur in the future does not invalidate our individual free will. Nor does it absolve us of the responsibility to make constructive choices in life. It does, however, give us the ability to prepare for changing conditions, as well as an appreciation of the rhythms of our own life.

Understanding our relationships

Using *synastry*, two people's horoscopes can be compared, and areas of compatibility and conflict can be assessed. Used in this way, astrology can enable us to understand our relationships in a broader context, and appreciate other people in our lives for what they are, rather than for what we would like them to be. We can acknowledge the needs, motivations and limitations of our partners, friends, family members or colleagues, whilst at the same time knowing our own more fully.

3

Choosing a Career

Knowing our own birthchart can also help us to make career choices. It can help us to identify our aptitudes and clarify the kind of work we want to do. For instance, do we prefer to work with people and, if so, as part of a team or in a leadership role? Do we prefer to work autonomously and be responsible for setting our own goals or do we prefer to be set clear targets by others? Are we good at dealing sensitively with the public? Would we prefer an active job involving physical activity or one that deals primarily with information? People tend to be happier and more successful doing work that matches not only their skills but also their personal preferences and their values.

The Rhythms of Life

As the planets orbit the Sun, they also orbit our birthchart, triggering changes within ourselves and in our lives as they contact different points within it. By being aware of the planetary dynamics operating in our birthcharts, we discover that our lives take place within a larger context of patterns and rhythms and that every phase in our life has a beginning, middle and an end. We can also get a better sense of how our present circumstances came about and what course of action would be to our best advantage.

Current affairs, news and political events are also given a new dimension, since many of the changes in the political landscape of the world are reflected in (or are perhaps a reflection of) the changing pattern of the planets. For instance, the passage of the planet Neptune through Capricorn from 1984 to 1998 saw an erosion of the solid political boundaries between the capitalist and communist worlds, which began with the coming to power of Mikhail Gorbachev in 1984 in the former USSR. Capricorn represents structure, be it political, social, economic or personal, whilst Neptune, like the sea, has an eroding or dissolving effect.

In 1989 there were major line-ups of planets that many astrologers foresaw as heralding significant world events. On 9 November, the

4

Berlin Wall was breached, only four days before an exact line-up of
Neptune with Saturn, which along with Venus had joined Uranus
and Neptune in Capricorn. Such a configuration occurs in Capricorn
only once, approximately, every 320 years and could be said to
represent the dissolving (Neptune) of state (Capricorn) boundaries
(Saturn). Jupiter was directly opposing Saturn as well, indicating the
benign (Jupiter) power of people acting together. Many of the other
major events of that year, including the massacre at Tiananmen
Square in Beijing, and the revolution in Romania, were reflected
exactly by the unfolding drama in the heavens.

Individuality and shared experience

Astrology enables us to appreciate and respect both our differences
from each other and our common humanity. It reveals the pattern of
our uniqueness, yet shows us that the elements of our experience
are the same the world over. We are all part of a much larger story
that is constantly evolving through time.

practice

Write a list of your ten best qualities (including skills and
aptitudes), then five qualities or aspects of your behaviour that
you would like to change. When you cast your own birthchart
using the techniques described later in this book, look at your list
again to see whether the qualities you wrote down are reflected in
the birthchart.

TIME, SPACE AND THE HOROSCOPE

A strology is based on the interpretation of horoscopes. A horoscope is, *in essence, a map of the solar system drawn up for a particular moment of time, usually that of an individual's birth (in which case it is called a birthchart), but it could equally well be the 'birth' of a business, a country or a project. In natal astrology, which is the prime focus of this book, the moment of time we are interested in is a person's birth. This moment (actually the moment of the baby's first breath) is the key to understanding the personality and destiny of that person.*

Before we can begin to look at the astrological meaning of a horoscope, we need to understand a little of how and why it is constructed the way it is. The aim of this chapter is to reveal a little of the astronomical background behind the horoscope and how to read its symbols.

Glyphs — an astrological shorthand

Glyphs (pictorial symbols) are used as astrological shorthand to represent the planets and signs of the zodiac. Most of the diagrams that follow will use the glyphs shown in the table below, so it is a good idea to commit them to memory, so that you can 'read' a horoscope fluently.

There are glyphs for each planet and each sign. In addition to the latter, its symbol or pictorial representation (based on the constellation with which it is associated) is shown. Suggested colours are also shown, although many astrologers use different colour schemes.

Planet	Colour	Glyph
Sun	Yellow	☉
Moon	Orange	☽
Mercury	Yellowy green	☿
Venus	Pink	♀
Mars	Red	♂
Jupiter	Royal blue	♃
Saturn	Navy blue	♄
Uranus	Purple	♅
Neptune	Violet	♆
Pluto	Turquoise	♀ or ♇
North Node of the Moon (Dragon's Head)*	Gold	☊
South Node of the Moon (Dragon's Tail)*	Grey	☋

Sign	Colour	Glyph	Symbol
Aries	Red	♈	Ram
Taurus	Pink	♉	Bull
Gemini	Pale pink	♊	Twins
Cancer	Orange	♋	Crab
Leo	Yellow	♌	Lion
Virgo	Yellowy green	♍	Virgin
Libra	Dark green	♎	Scales
Scorpio	Turquoise	♏	Scorpion
Sagittarius	Royal blue	♐	Centaur/ Archer
Capricorn	Navy blue	♑	Goat
Aquarius	Purple	♒	Water-bearer
Pisces	Violet	♓	Fishes

Note that the North and South Nodes of the Moon are not heavenly bodies but abstract points formed by the intersection of the ecliptic (see over) with the path of the Moon.

Note also that in the table above, the Sun and Moon are listed under 'planets'. This is another astrological shorthand and one that makes sceptics assume that astrologers are unaware of basic astronomy. The Sun is a star, not a planet, and the Moon is a moon, or body orbiting a planet. However, it is easier if we sometimes describe them as planets, so we will follow this convention.

PRACTICE

Practise drawing the glyphs for each planet and sign, then test whether you can identify them by referring to the above table.

The astronomy of time and space

We all know that the Sun is the centre of the solar system and that the Earth orbits the Sun, not vice versa. However, astrology is a *geocentric*, or Earth-centred system, so the Sun, Moon and planets are plotted on to a horoscope in the positions they appear to occupy as seen from Earth. Again, this is not an error by astronomically challenged astrologers, rather it reflects the fact that, being human beings, our reference point is naturally our planet of birth.

If we look at the night sky repeatedly over a period of several weeks, we see stars and constellations, those patterns of stars that we can readily identify such as Pegasus or the Great Bear (known also as the Plough or Big Dipper). Although the stars appear to move due to the daily rotation of the Earth around its own axis and its yearly orbit of the Sun, they also appear static relative to each other. The Moon and the planets, however, appear to travel across the sky against the background of the stars, roughly in line with an arc called the *ecliptic*, which is the *apparent* path of the Sun around the Earth (Figure 1).

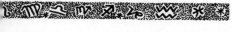

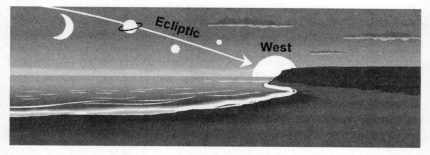

Figure 1 The ecliptic (path of the Sun) with the Moon and planets on or near it

Although not essential to an understanding of astrology, it is an enriching experience to look at the sky over successive evenings and watch the planets gradually travelling around the zodiac. The best time to see the planets is around sunset before the stars make their appearance. Depending on where the planets are in the zodiac, on a clear evening Mercury, Venus, Mars, Jupiter and Saturn may be seen with the naked eye, reminding us that astrology is a *living* art that links us with all life and the cosmos beyond.

The twelve signs of the zodiac

The ecliptic is divided into twelve sectors, known as the *signs of the zodiac*. There are twelve 'zodiac signs' from Aries to Pisces. Rather than use the *sidereal* (starry) zodiac of the twelve visible constellations (named Aries, Taurus, etc.), Western astrologers, perhaps confusingly, use the *tropical* zodiac. This is based on the position of the Sun (viewed from Earth) at the *Vernal Equinox*, that time of year (around 21 March) when day and night are equal in length. This point is designated 0° Aries, i.e. the starting point of the 360° wheel of the zodiac (Figure 2).

The zodiac is circular, and each zodiac sign occupies 30° of that circle. The positions of the planets relative to the zodiac signs give

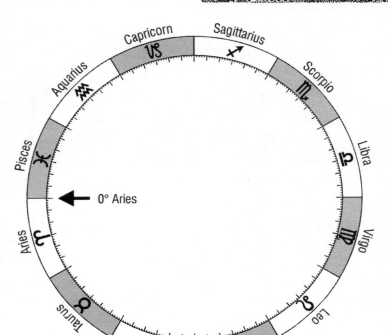

Figure 2 The twelve signs of the zodiac

us a co-ordinate system that we can use to identify exactly where a planet is located in the sky and, hence, to map them on to the horoscope. Each zodiac sign is marked 0°–29°. For instance, in Figure 3, which shows a small section of a horoscope (like a slice from a pie), we can see that the Sun (☉) is in the 12th degree of the sign Aries. Note that from the beginning of a sign (0°) to the start of the following sign, we have moved in an anticlockwise direction.

Planets move at different speeds usually in an anticlockwise direction around the zodiac. For example, the Sun moves about one degree per day (so taking 30 days to travel through a zodiac sign), whilst the Moon moves approximately 13 degrees per day (taking just over two days to travel through a complete sign).

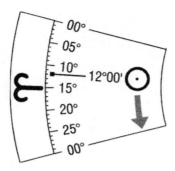

Figure 3 Pie-slice of a typical horoscope, showing the Sun at 12° Aries

Using an *ephemeris* (a book of tables showing the daily positions of the planets), we can plot the positions of the Sun, Moon and planets on to the horoscope. When you begin to cast, or calculate, your first horoscope, you will need various items, including an ephemeris. Alternatively, you can choose from a range of astrological computer software, or even use the Internet (see Chapter 5).

The Houses of the Horoscope

Knowing the positions of the planets relative to the signs of the zodiac at the moment of birth can be equated with knowing the person's character. To find out how that character manifests in everyday life, we need to know the positions of the *twelve Houses*. The twelve Houses are a further twelve-fold subdivision of the horoscope that symbolise different areas of a person's life such as home and family life, career, friendships, etc. (Figure 4).

The Houses also correlate the moment of birth with the geographical location of birth.

11

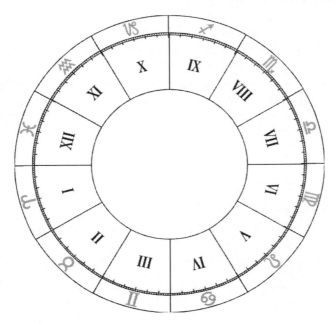

Figure 4 The twelve Houses, using the Equal House system

CALCULATING THE ASCENDANT

To determine the positions of the Houses we first need to know the part of the zodiac that was rising above the eastern horizon. Due to the Earth's daily rotation around its own axis (which gives us day and night), approximately every two hours a different sign of the zodiac will rise in the east. The degree of the sign that is rising is called the *Ascendant* (Asc), the sign itself is called the *Rising Sign*. The Ascendant symbolises our outward persona – the face we present to the world most readily, and also our body type, physical appearance and our relationship to our immediate environment.

Because the Ascendant moves approximately 1° every 4 minutes (reflecting the rotation of the Earth), it is important to know a person's exact birth time. A difference of four minutes could mean

that the Ascendant will be in a different sign, therefore indicative of quite a different personality and body type. To calculate the Ascendant and House cusps one must also know the place of birth, preferably to within a couple of miles.

To visualise the movement of the planets and Houses around the birthchart, imagine the Houses whizzing round rapidly anticlockwise (corresponding to the daily rotation of the Earth) and the planets moving round more sedately, but still anticlockwise.

Marking the House cusps

On the horoscope, the Ascendant is the starting point for the twelve Houses, and is the *cusp*, or starting point, of the Ist House. Each House cusp is marked by a series of lines radiating out from the centre of the horoscope, and the cusps of Houses I to VI (by convention the Houses are marked using roman numerals) are always directly opposite the cusps for Houses VII to XII respectively. The Ascendant is always shown on the left of the horoscope, the Ascendant/Descendant axis marking the position of the horizon at birth (Figure 5).

The angles

Whilst the Ascendant represents the eastern horizon, where the Sun and planets rise, the *Descendant* (its opposite point, the cusp of the VIIth House) represents the western horizon, where the Sun and planets set. The Descendant symbolises 'significant others' in one's life, often the marriage or business partner. The point of the ecliptic highest overhead is called the *Midheaven* (or MC, an abbreviation of the Latin *Medium Coeli*). The Midheaven (in unequal House systems) is the cusp of the Xth House, and is always opposite the lowest point (or nadir), called the *IC* (from the Latin *Immum Coeli*), which is the cusp of the IVth House. The Midheaven symbolises our public (rather than our everyday) persona and how we wish to be perceived by society as a whole, whilst the IC symbolises our private life, roots and family. The Ascendant, IC, Descendant and Midheaven are called the *angles*, and can be likened to East, North, West and South

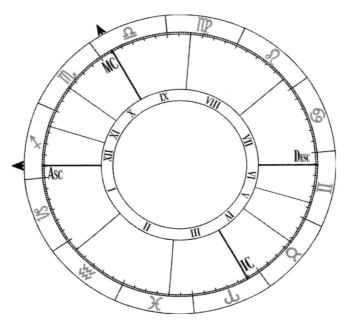

Figure 5 Typical House cusps (using a non-equal house system) and angles

respectively. The Ascendant is the most significant angle in astrological interpretation. Note that north is at the bottom of the horoscope and south at the top!

Different house systems

As in many areas of astrology, there are competing techniques and systems, and the Houses of the horoscope are no exception. Some astrologers use the *Equal House* method, which simply divides the horoscope into twelve equal Houses, starting at the Ascendant. Thus if the Ascendant were at 26° Aries, then the cusp of the second House would be at 26° Taurus, the cusp of the third at 26° Gemini and so on. This book uses the unequal *Placidus* House system, as tables of Houses using this system are commonly available. The reader is invited to experiment with different House systems at a later stage.

The aspects

Once the planets and the Houses have been plotted on the horoscope, we can see what *aspects* the planets and angles, form with each other. Aspects are specific angular relationships between individual planets (including the Asc and MC) that describe the nature of their relationship. These are either *flowing* or *dynamic* (easy or challenging). They reflect the division of the circle of the horoscope by different numbers, for instance the *opposition* is produced by dividing the horoscope in two (180°). The most commonly used aspects are shown below.

Aspect	Angle	Glyph	Relationship	Division of circle	Colour of aspect lines on horoscope
Conjunction	0°	☌	Flowing or Dynamic	1	Red or green dashed circle
Opposition	180°	☍	Dynamic	2	Red
Trine	120°	△	Flowing	3	Green
Square	90°	□	Dynamic	4	Red
Sextile	60°	✳	Flowing	6	Green

Thus, if the Sun is at 10° Aries and the Moon is at 10° Leo, they are *trine* to each other (shorthand for saying they are 120° from each other), and so are in a flowing, harmonious relationship with each other. If instead, the Moon were at 10° Cancer, they would be *square* to each other, meaning that there would be a tension between them or that the head (Sun) and heart (Moon) would be pulling in different directions.

The aspects are drawn in the centre of the wheel, using red or green lines depending on the nature of the aspect. The sextile and trine are green, the square and opposition red. Conjunctions and *stelliums* (multiple conjunctions) are usually marked by dotted red or dotted green lines around the planets involved (the colour depending on whether the planets blend or conflict with each other).

ORBS

Obviously, two planets will rarely form an *exact* aspect, so an *orb* is allowed either side of the planets involved, within which an aspect can be said to occur. Using the above example, if the Moon were at 18° Leo, the Moon and the Sun would still be in trine but only just. The Sun, Moon, Ascendant and Midheaven have wider orbs due to their importance, as do conjunctions, trines and oppositions. Typical orbs are reproduced below.

Planet	Max. orb	Aspect	Max. orb	Aspect	Max. orb
Sun, Moon Ascendant, Midheaven	8°	Conjunction	8°	Trine	8°
Mercury, Venus, Mars, Jupiter, Saturn	5°	Sextile	5°	Opposition	8°
Uranus, Neptune, Pluto, Moon's Nodes	3°	Square	5°		

Note that the orbs given are the **maximum** allowed, so for instance a trine between Uranus and Neptune would be allowable only if they were within 3° of an exact trine, i.e. between 117° and 123° of each other. The more exact the aspect, the stronger is its influence. With two planets whose maximum orbs are different, use the greater orb. For instance, in an opposition aspect between the Ascendant and Pluto, the allowable orb is 8°.

A situation in which planets can be treated as being in aspect to each other, even though not within the allowable orbs, is when a third planet aspects both. For instance, say Mercury is at 2° Leo, conjunct Venus at 6° Leo. Saturn, at 8° 30′ Sagittarius, trines Venus. Although Saturn is 126° from Mercury (i.e. beyond the maximum orb of 5° for an aspect of Mercury), it is still in aspect to it by virtue of Mercury's conjunction with Venus.

AN EXAMPLE HOROSCOPE

Figure 6 is an example horoscope, that of Jimi Hendrix born at 10:15 a.m. Pacific War Time, on 27 November 1942, Seattle, Washington, USA. (Source: Edwin Steinbrecher Data Collection: see Appendix 1.)

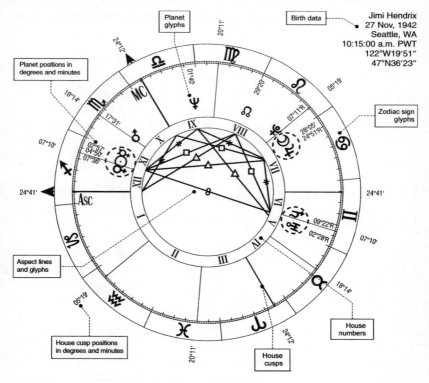

Figure 6 Example horoscope of Jimi Hendrix

PRACTICE

To get used to drawing up horoscopes, copy the above example, using the blank chartwheel in Chapter 5. Use colours for the planets and zodiac sign glyphs to enhance the symbolism.

3 ELEMENTS OF INTERPRETATION

Nobody can claim to know the mechanism by which one's personality is 'fixed' at the moment of birth, but in the experience of many thousands of astrologers throughout the ages, it seems to 'work'. The aim of this chapter is to familiarise you with the symbols used in astrology so that you can 'read' a horoscope and understand its basic elements.

INTERPRETING THE TWELVE SIGNS OF THE ZODIAC

We have seen that the signs of the zodiac are a useful co-ordinate system by which to locate the positions of the planets, but their importance in astrology extends beyond this function. The twelve signs of the zodiac represent different **qualities of experience**, and alter, or colour, the way planets contained within them operate. Thus Aries, the first sign, symbolises self-assertion, energy and personality, and in a horoscope any planet found in Aries will consequently operate in a forceful and dynamic manner. For example, a person born with **Mercury** (symbolising the faculty of speech and communication) in **Aries** will, in general, communicate directly, assertively and confidently. You always know where you stand with Mercury in Aries!

The four elements

Each sign is governed by one of four *Elements*: Fire, Air, Water and Earth. These are also known as *triplicities*. The Fire signs, Aries, Leo

and Sagittarius, are energetic, expressive and outward moving in their energy. The Air signs, Gemini, Libra and Aquarius, are communicative, sociable and rational. The Water signs, Cancer, Scorpio and Pisces, are emotional, flowing and reflective, whilst the Earth signs, Taurus, Virgo and Capricorn, are connected with the physical world, the senses and the practical world of work and achievement.

A horoscope with a predominance or lack of planets (including the Asc and MC) in one Element tells you something about the person. For instance, a predominance of Fire indicates energy, vitality and confidence. Too much Fire, though, and you get egotism, over-dramatisation and attention seeking. Too little and you may have someone who lacks vitality or any 'spark'.

An abundance of Air, on the other hand, indicates intelligence, popularity and communication skills, whilst too much can correspond to either a social-butterfly mentality or to 'living in the head'. Too little Air and there is often a lack of objectivity or a mistrust of words.

An abundance of Water indicates emotional sensitivity, warmth and the capacity for closeness. Too much and you tend to get over-sensitivity, neuroses and dependency, whilst with too little there is the possibility of coldness or a fear of intimacy.

A predominance of Earth in a horoscope is a sign of many practical skills, common sense and financial prudence. With too much Earth there is often a materialistic, blinkered outlook on life. If there is a lack of Earth in a horoscope, the individual may find establishing financial stability difficult, or may lack common sense.

Mode

Three modes, or *quadruplicities*, also govern signs. The *Cardinal* signs, Aries, Cancer, Libra and Capricorn, are active and initiatory; the four *Fixed* signs, Taurus, Leo, Scorpio and Aquarius, are stable and sustaining; the four *Mutable* signs, Gemini, Virgo, Sagittarius and Pisces are changeable and mediating in their energies.

Again, noting a predominance or lack of a particular mode can be useful. A predominance of Cardinal signs can correspond to someone who is active, dynamic and achievement-orientated, but who finds it difficult to relax or slow down.

A predominance of planets in Fixed signs may indicate someone who is slow to make decisions or changes in life, but tends to stick to a particular path or set of attitudes with great determination.

With Mutable signs predominating, there may be great flexibility and an abundance of social skills, but also a tendency to indecisiveness or aimlessness.

POLARITY

Each sign also has a polarity, positive or negative, which can be likened to yang and yin, masculine and feminine, extrovert and introvert (but not 'good' and 'bad') respectively. Positive signs are

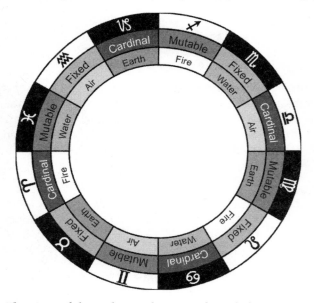

Figure 7 The signs of the zodiac: polarity, mode and element

more outward moving and active, whilst negative signs are more inward moving and passive in their energy. A birthchart with a marked imbalance of one polarity over another may indicate extroversion or introversion, especially if other factors in the chart support this view, such as the sign position of the Sun, Moon and ASC.

In Figure 7, signs in white are positive, signs in black are negative. Thus Aquarius is a positive, Fixed Air sign, whilst Virgo is a negative, Mutable Earth sign. There follows a brief description of each of the twelve signs.

♈ ARIES

Aries brings qualities of energy, dynamism, personality, drive and directness to any planet located within it. It operates in an overt and open manner, but can be headstrong and quick-tempered. People with several planets in Aries are likely to be forceful, assertive and competitive.

♉ TAURUS

Taurus energy is stable, calm and oriented towards the world of the senses. It builds things up patiently, be it a business, a relationship or a garden. Material security, as represented by money and possessions, and the physical pleasures of sex, food and drink, are all part of Taurus' domain. Several planets in Taurus can indicate someone who is practical, business-like and endowed with common sense.

♊ GEMINI

Gemini is changeable, mobile, communicative and sociable. It loves the stimulation of interchange between people, be it through talking or the written word. Easily bored, Gemini seeks variety and dislikes doing any one thing for too long. An emphasis on Gemini indicates someone who is intelligent, curious, friendly and often youthful.

♋ CANCER

Cancer is emotional, nurturing and protective, and planets in this sign operate in a sensitive manner. There is a love of home and family, as well as of tradition and the past generally. Cancer can at times be defensive and may put up a protective shell. An emphasis on Cancer reflects someone who is caring, supportive and who seeks emotional security.

♌ LEO

Leo is self-expressive, proud and dramatic. Leo loves to impress by acting with flair and confidence. At times attention-seeking, those with an emphasis in Leo are often good at entertaining others. Love affairs, play and creativity are often emphasised in the lives of people with several planets in this sign. Leadership and children also come under Leo's dominion.

♍ VIRGO

Virgo is analytical, orderly and helpful. It discriminates between what is fine and gross, and acts with precision and skill. Purity is an important concept to Virgo and this may extend to an interest in diet, health and morality, through may manifest also as prudishness or a critical nature. Several planets in Virgo suggests someone who has practical skills and a fine sense of judgement.

♎ LIBRA

Libra is balanced, sociable and attractive. It seeks harmony in all things, including relationships, and has good taste and an appreciation for beauty. It is eager to please and be accepted by others. Popularity, attractiveness and cultural sophistication are often found where a birthchart has several planets in this sign.

♏ SCORPIO

Scorpio is intense, strong-willed and transformative. It seeks to penetrate to the underlying realities of any situation and is thus drawn to psychology, detective work and mysteries of any kind. Having several planets in Scorpio indicates a strong sexuality, personal power, and a need to periodically let go of the past and find new life.

♐ SAGITTARIUS

Sagittarius is expansive, optimistic and adventurous. It sees life as an endless journey of discovery and is eager to learn new ideas and explore other cultures. An emphasis on Sagittarius indicates someone who is good-humoured, broad-minded and philosophical.

♑ CAPRICORN

Capricorn is structured, focused and professional. It sets goals, makes plans and patiently but determinedly sets out to achieve them. Work, business and career are natural outlets for Capricorn energy, and those with an emphasis in this sign tend to gravitate towards positions of authority and responsibility.

♒ AQUARIUS

Aquarius is innovative, radical and sociable. Sometimes eccentric, it seeks affiliations with those of like mind and is often ahead of its time. Equality and freedom are important principles for Aquarius, and those with an emphasis in this sign are likely to be progressive, humane and unconventional.

♓ PISCES

Pisces is imaginative, compassionate and universal. It seeks to transcend everyday reality and enter a realm of oneness and

non-duality. Art, music and spirituality, as well as alcohol and drugs, are manifestations of this impulse. Pisces absorbs feelings and emotions like a sponge, and tends to be sensitive and impressionable. An emphasis on Pisces can give rise to a kindly or artistic nature.

Below is a keyword table for quick reference, describing the essential qualities of each sign, together with the corresponding part of the body to which the signs relates.

Sign	Quality	Bodily correspondence
Aries	Self-assertion, energy, personality	Head, face, brain
Taurus	Stability, financial security, material resources	Neck, throat
Gemini	Communication, mobility, versatility	Hands, arms, lungs
Cancer	Feeling, emotional security, home and family	Chest, womb, stomach, breasts
Leo	Self-expression, youth, love	Heart, back
Virgo	Analysis, work, health	Intestines
Libra	Relationships, beauty, balance	Kidneys
Scorpio	Intensity, passion, transformation	Genitals, excretory system
Sagittarius	Belief, freedom, expansion	Hips, thighs
Capricorn	Realism, business, boundaries	Knees, skeleton, bones
Aquarius	Freedom, modernism, friendship	Calves, shins, ankles
Pisces	Universality, receptivity, imagination	Feet

The planets

Each planet (including Sun, Moon and Moon's Nodes) corresponds to a specific **psychological function** to be found in human beings. For instance, Mercury symbolises the mind and how we think and

communicate, whilst the Moon symbolises our emotions, self-image and how we relate to our mother (or most nurturing parent). The function symbolised by each planet is always coloured and qualified by the sign and House in which it is located in the horoscope. Though representing a part of one's own make-up, planets can also be projected on to the outside world, especially other people.

The Sun, Moon, Mercury, Venus and Mars are called the *personal planets* as they indicate factors that relate to the personality and personal life of the individual.

Jupiter and Saturn are called the *social planets* because they indicate how the individual relates to the larger society of which he or she is a part (as does the Midheaven).

Uranus, Neptune and Pluto are called the *trans-Saturnians* or *outer planets*. These are slower moving and tend to stay in a sign for a long period, and thus have a greater influence on the generation in which the individual was born rather than the individual himself or herself. The exception is when an individual has several aspects to the outer planets from the Ascendant, Midheaven or personal planets.

Rulerships

Planet	Rulership	Detriment
Sun	Leo	Aquarius
Moon	Cancer	Capricorn
Mercury	Gemini, Virgo	Sagittarius, Pisces
Venus	Taurus, Libra	Scorpio, Aries
Mars	Aries, Scorpio	Libra, Taurus
Jupiter	Sagittarius, Pisces	Gemini, Virgo
Saturn	Capricorn, Aquarius	Cancer, Leo
Uranus	Aquarius	Leo
Neptune	Pisces	Virgo
Pluto	Scorpio	Taurus

Traditionally, each planet relates to a particular sign, which is said to 'rule' it, i.e. be in sympathy with it. Likewise, planets can be in 'detriment' if they are in a sign inimical to their nature.

Some traditional astrologers dispute the rulerships of the three outer planets, Uranus, Neptune and Pluto, since they have been discovered only relatively recently (1781, 1846 and 1930 respectively). With signs having dual rulerships, these astrologers would argue that one should take note of the traditional ruler first.

Ruler of the Ascendant

The planet that rules the sign on the Ascendant (Rising Sign) is called the *Ruler of the Ascendant,* and together with its sign, House position and aspects it tells us much about the nature of our outward personality and in what area of our lives we invest our energies. For instance, if an individual has Virgo Rising, look at the sign and House position of Mercury. This is the 'Ruler of the Ascendant' and can tell you about the life of the individual in general terms. For instance, to use the previous example, if Mercury is in Pisces and the IIIrd House, you might expect the person to be notably poetic, imaginative and good at communicating intuitive insights to others.

Retrograde planets

From our geocentric viewpoint, the planets can occasionally be seen to be slowing, stopping and then going backwards! Obviously, this is not really happening, it just appears so from the Earth because we ourselves are going around the Sun. This is called *retrograde motion* (the glyph for which is R_x). Normal, 'forward' movement is called *direct motion*, the glyph for which is D. In the ephemeris, the starting date of a planet's retrograde motion is marked with the R_x glyph. When the planet turns direct again, the D glyph is shown. In some ephemerides, grey shading is used to mark clearly the period of retrograde motion.

Astrologically, retrograde planets are said to operate in a very internalised, cautious manner. For instance, if someone has Jupiter retrograde in their birthchart, they may live by a set of clear internal aims and beliefs that are at odds with those of most other people. To give another example, Mercury retrograde may indicate a person who thinks carefully before he or she speaks, and whose perceptions are often highly individualistic or surprising. When Mercury goes retrograde during the year, one can often expect postal delays, communication breakdowns and misunderstandings, although it is an excellent time for personal reflection, brainstorming or making plans.

The Moon's Nodes retrograde around the zodiac, except for brief periods of direct motion.

Below is a keyword table for quick reference, which describes each of the planets.

Planet	Psychological function
Sun	Ego, conscious self, essential approach to life
Moon	Emotions, feelings, inner self
Mercury	Mind, communication, speech
Venus	Relationship, attraction, pleasure
Mars	Self-assertion, will, sex
Jupiter	Optimism, growth, opportunity
Saturn	Realism, concentration, discipline
Uranus	Individuality, freedom, higher mind
Neptune	Soul, imagination, compassion
Pluto	Instincts, urge to survive, will to power
Moon's North Node	Capacity for personal growth, fulfilment of inner potential
Moon's South Node	Stagnation, decay

Chiron, a planetoid (or 'Centaur'), discovered in 1977, is also used by some astrologers.

Planets in signs

Following this section are tables giving keywords for planets in each sign. Note that some planets are described as feminine, some as masculine. Astrologers believe that as individuals we each have access to qualities that are traditionally described as 'feminine' and 'masculine'. A woman with a well-aspected Mars in Aries, for instance, is likely to be assertive, dynamic and outspoken, whilst a man with Moon in Cancer may be notably caring, home loving and supportive of others. Astrology allows one to see through simple stereotypes based on gender, sexuality, class or race, and honours people's complexity and individuality.

PRACTICE

Whilst reading the keywords below, imagine other ways in which a planet can manifest in a sign of the zodiac, based on your own understanding of yourself and other people.

SUN

The Sun symbolises the *essential self*, the *will, consciousness, the ego, objectivity, individuality, wholeness* and the *spirit*. It is the masculine principle in contradistinction to that symbolised by the Moon. It is personified by *rulers, leaders, public figures, the famous* and *personalities*.

In the horoscope, it is the point where we shine and are most ourselves. It also symbolises how we experience our own father (or dominant parent). The sign and House in which it is found, together with the aspects it makes to other planets, show our primary orientation towards life, the area of life in which we put forth our best energies, and how our ego integrates with the rest of our psyche.

☉ ♈	Assertive; energetic; combative; leading; impatient; sporty; brave; enterprising; tough; outspoken; competitive; impulsive; loves winning.
☉ ♉	Persevering; practical; materialistic; seeks security; physical; obstinate; pleasure-loving; moneyed; patient; business skills; grounded; loves providing.
☉ ♊	Articulate; clever; nervous; friendly; funny; many interests; changeable; superficial; verbal; sociable; witty; adaptable; mobile; loves communication.
☉ ♋	Warm; caring; emotional; parental; homely; deep feelings; emotional depth; familial; sensitive; hard shell; protective; private; loves nurturing.
☉ ♌	Confident; self-assured; proud; creative; egotistical; bossy; fun; dominating; acting; theatrical; vain; child-like; loves self-expression.
☉ ♍	Intelligent; discriminating; orderly; critical; methodical; skilled; healing; service; detail; analysis; healthy; anxious; self-critical; loves perfecting.
☉ ♎	Attractive; balanced; harmonious; charming; sociable; refined; unreliable; cultured; seeks approval; artistic; social skills; loves relationships.
☉ ♏	Passionate; strong-willed; forceful; sexual; taboo; magnetic; jealous; investigative; penetrating, psychological depth; survival; loves intensity.
☉ ♐	Freedom loving; optimistic; philosophical; undisciplined; fun-loving; adventurous; questing; well-travelled; outspoken; scattered; noble; loves truth.
☉ ♑	Hard-working; ambitious; goal-orientated; egocentric; inhibited; dutiful; inflexible; pragmatic; respected; organising; seeks status; loves achievement.
☉ ♒	Sociable; humanitarian; seeks knowledge; political; progressive; radical; intellectual; unconventional; modern; eccentric; rebellious; loves freedom.
☉ ♓	Compassionate; imaginative; sensitive; dreamy; spiritual; addictive; empathetic; open; loving; visionary; seeks to heal; loves transcendence.

MOON

The Moon symbolises *feelings, emotions, the home and family life, the self image, nurturing, protection* and *the unconscious mind*. It represents the feminine principle, and complements the Sun. It is personified by *wives, mothers, women, supportive figures* and *those who protect.*

In the horoscope it is the point that reveals what makes us feel most secure and the qualities, activities or things that we need in order to feel good about ourselves and to have a more flowing response to life.

It also symbolises how we experience our own mother (or most nurturing parent) and the type of home life we create. The sign and House in which it is found, together with the aspects the Moon makes to other planets, show our unconscious orientation towards life, the area of life in which we are most at home and how our feelings are integrated with the rest of the psyche.

☽ ♈	Assertive; volatile; restless; hasty; energetic; primal; impatient; rebellious; independent; needs activity; irritable; passionate.
☽ ♉	Emotionally constant; pleasure-loving; needs financial security; lazy; placid; comfortable; sensual; seeks physical affection; food and wine; domestic tranquillity.
☽ ♊	Talkative; inconstant; changeable; good mimic; witty; nervous; mobile; gossip; reading and writing; needs stimulation and exchange.
☽ ♋	Sensitive; caring; deep feelings; receptive; attachments; familial; the past; nostalgic; parental; protective; needs emotional security.
☽ ♌	Dramatic; self-aggrandising; confident; child-like; fun; intuitive creativity; generous; bossy; authoritarian; seeks attention; needs respect.
☽ ♍	Emotionally cool; critical; constructive; practical; articulate; reserved; exacting; meticulous; analyses feelings; needs order.
☽ ♎	Sociable; loving; affectionate; refined; tasteful; unreliable; seeks relationship; friendly; diplomatic; emotionally balanced; needs harmony.
☽ ♏	Emotionally intense; controlled; extreme; possessive; powerful mother; self-destructive; passionate; hides feelings; survival instinct; needs intimacy.
☽ ♐	Jovial; good-humoured; frank; open; restless; idealistic; optimistic; well-travelled; home abroad; loves learning; needs meaning.
☽ ♑	Responsible; mature; reserved; undemonstrative; practical; cautious; hard-working; inhibited; reliable; professional; needs achievement.
☽ ♒	Friendly; humanitarian; detached; idealistic; sociable; group-orientated; unusual home-life; modern; progressive parenting; needs freedom.
☽ ♓	Sensitive; emotionally open; escapist; dreamy; romantic; artistic; spiritual; shy; reclusive; imaginative; compassionate; needs transcendence.

ASCENDANT (ASC)

The Ascendant symbolises the *personality, appearance, body type, mask, environment, surroundings* and *birth circumstances*. It is the part of us that is most readily shown to (or seen by) the outside world. Its sign position and the aspects it makes to the planets in the horoscope show the nature of our outward personality and physical appearance, and how they are integrated with the rest of the psyche.

ASC ♈	Strong personality; assertive; energetic; surface confidence; aggressive; fighting; strong-willed; pushy; bold; rash; impulsive; front; extroverted; lively; decisive; spirited; youthful. Body type and appearance: tall; reddish or blonde hair; strong forehead; wiry or curly hair; blonde or reddish hair; strong or compact frame; bulging or staring eyes; hats.
ASC ♉	Placid personality; practical; sensible; sensual; solid; earthy; undemonstrative; stable; stubborn; secure; hedonistic; slow; deliberate; persistent; tactile; comfortable; materialistic. Body type and appearance: attractive; heavy; not tall; sexy; chubby; animal grace; soft skin; rounded features; thick neck; dark hair; fleshy; natural textiles.
ASC ♊	Bright personality; talkative; friendly; changeable; lively; adaptable; quick; superficial; mobile; intellectual; youthful; fun-loving; communicative; witty; well-read; verbal; fluent. Body type and appearance: tall; light hair; expressive hands; bony; long-limbed; hazel eyes; quick movements; youthful appearance; bright or fun clothes; spectacles.
ASC ♋	Sensitive personality; caring; warm; emotional; sympathetic; motherly; shy; dependent; home-loving; crabby; instinctive; hospitable; protective; secure; reflective. Body type and appearance: pale skin; soft, rounded features; dark hair; grey eyes; short stature; large upper body; fluid movements; soft clothes; blue or dark colours.
ASC ♌	Confident personality; extrovert; magnanimous; egotistical; leading; acting; fun-loving; regal; dramatic; proud; dignified; strong will; creative; sunny; self-respecting; childlike. Body type and appearance: tall stature; commanding presence; sunny face; mane of hair; fair hair; ruddy complexion; upright; dramatic clothes; impressive; yellow, orange and gold.

ASC ♍	Reserved personality; quiet; perfectionist; critical; practical; hardworking; efficient; orderly; helpful; anxious; analytical; organised; thoughtful; modest; cool; intellectual; humble. Body type and appearance: slender; wiry; pale complexion; healthy-looking; delicate features; natural; dark-haired; tidy; neat clothes; natural textiles; earth colours.
ASC ♎	Attractive personality; charming; sociable; popular; stylish; sweet; balanced; vain; friendly; obliging; good manners; refined; co-operative; graceful; harmonious; cultured. Body type and appearance: tall; attractive; clear complexion; good features; round or oval face; blue/grey eyes; light hair; fashionable clothes; colour co-ordinated.
ASC ♏	Powerful personality; strong-willed; intense; passionate; reserved; secretive; magnetic; untiring; compulsive; sexy; hidden depths; destructive; resourceful; insightful; controlled. Body type and appearance: robust; dusky or dark complexion; penetrating eyes; strong face; dark hair/eyes; powerful presence; dark clothing; leather; maroons; bottle greens.
ASC ♐	Outgoing personality; expansive; good-humoured; friendly; messy; athletic; confident; positive; active; enthusiastic; open; frank; honest; well-travelled; principled; easygoing. Body type and appearance: tall; ruddy/sunburnt complexion; long face; strong; open face; fair hair; casual clothes; sportswear; purples; bright colours.
ASC ♑	Serious personality; ambitious; undemonstrative; pragmatic; assiduous; respectable; inhibited; goal-conscious; professional; responsible; realistic; cautious; business-like; wise. Body type and appearance: tall; dark hair; bony; long neck; gaunt; stern or downcast expression; classical or formal attire; tailored; smart; power-dressing; restrained colours: navy blue, grey, cream, black and white.
ASC ♒	Individualistic personality; friendly; sociable; progressive; humane; intellectual; radical; eccentric; exciting; detached; cool; unconventional; wacky; modern; independent; rebellious. Body type and appearance: tall; clear eyes; bright colours; striking; light hair; bony; tribal clothing; patterns; futuristic look; shocking; zigzags; unusual colour combinations.
ASC ♓	Dreamy personality; quiet; receptive; artistic; vague; passive; spiritual; unconfident; lonely; self-sacrificial; empathetic; imaginative; shy; amorphous; romantic; gentle. Body type and appearance: slender or short and heavy; pale; dark, shaggy hair; delicate; sleepy or bedroom eyes; amorphous features; loose clothing; sea-colours; unco-ordinated.

MERCURY

Mercury symbolises *communication, thinking, intelligence, mediation, logic, adaptability, mobility, reason, analysis, discrimination, humour, knowledge* and *speech*. Unlike the Sun and Moon, it is a neutral planet and is personified by *siblings, friends, young people, thinkers, writers, talkers* and *messengers*.

In the horoscope, Mercury shows how we communicate and think. It also symbolises mobility, telephone calls, magazines, messages, words and other forms of communication.

The sign and House in which it is found, together with the aspects Mercury makes to other planets, show the manner and style in which we communicate with others. Mercury's sign and House also show the area of life in (or about) which we are most communicative and intelligently detached, and how our powers of speech and mind are integrated with the rest of the psyche.

☿ ♈	Outspoken; quick-thinking; argumentative; decisive; precocious; mentally confident; rash; loud; enthusiastic; abrupt; jumps to conclusions.
☿ ♉	Thorough; dogmatic; patient; sensible; logical; organised; slow; loves books; business skills; negotiation; accountancy.
☿ ♊	Communicative; versatile; fluent; informed; intellectual; superficial; quick wit; curious; writing skills; mobile; sociable; short journeys.
☿ ♋	Subjective; good memory; subjective; sensitive communication; writing; reading; traditional; thinking about the past; good listener.
☿ ♌	Strong-minded; imaginative; entertaining; humorous; dramatic delivery; fixed opinions; teaching children; storytelling; creative writing.
☿ ♍	Analytical; diligent; practical; precise; efficient; reading and writing; orderly mind; critical; categorisation; calligraphy; intellectual.
☿ ♎	Reasonable; balanced mentality; diplomatic; adjusting to others' thinking; charming speech; co-operative; bland; cultured; fair; impartial.
☿ ♏	Penetrating intellect; secretive; sarcastic; acid; insightful; sharp; investigative; scheming; researching; puzzles; mysteries; un-foolable.
☿ ♐	Broadminded; philosophical; well-read; scattered mentality; dogmatic; idealistic; literary; preaching; frank; educated; broadcasting; writing, teaching.

☿ ♑	Serious; organised mind; thorough; logical; conservative ideas; realistic; shrewd; planning; patient; learns by experience; study; business skills.
☿ ♒	Progressive mind; inventive; unorthodox ideas; reforming; abstract; scientific; objective; mentally stimulated; experimental; information technology.
☿ ♓	Imaginative; vague; poetic; visualisation; intuitive; irrational; receptive; the unconscious mind; confused; non-verbal communications; subtle.

VENUS

Venus symbolises *relationship, harmony, love, attraction, art, beauty, pleasure, relaxation, friends* and *sex*. It is the 'feminine' principle of attraction and eroticism, as distinct from the 'masculine' principle of assertion and desire represented by Mars. In a man's chart Venus sometimes represents an ideal feminine image that gives rise to attraction to those who embody it or who evoke the qualities contained in it. It is personified by *young women artists, lovers, musicians, dancers, attractive people* and *diplomats*.

In the horoscope, it is the point that reveals what gives us pleasure and how we relate to others. Its sign, House position, and the aspects it makes to other planets show the type and quality of our relationships, the area of life in which we have a sense of well-being and satisfaction, and how our capacity to relate is integrated with the rest of the psyche.

♀ ♈	Outgoing; sociable; popular; brash; loud; sexy; fun-loving; rock and roll; ardent; passionate; stormy relationships; dynamic creativity.
♀ ♉	Pleasure loving; art and beauty; loyal; possessive; natural; sensual; good voice; love of luxury; food and wine; physically affectionate; sensuous art.
♀ ♊	Charming; flirtatious; light-hearted; friendly; witty; courteous; superficial; artful conversationalist; poetry; literature; writing; enjoys mobility.
♀ ♋	Loving; caring; enjoys parenting; domestic; affectionate; sensitive; tender; love of home; romantic; cherishing; cooking; hospitable.
♀ ♌	Expressive; artistic; theatrical; extravagant; creative; loves acting; outgoing affection; loyal; fun-loving; snobbish; regal; pompous; likes children.

♀ ♍	Discriminating in love; cool; refined; modest; service; friends at work; restrained; craft skills; love of detail; aesthetic criticism; delicate touch.
♀ ♎	Attractive; charming; flattery; artistic; popular; graceful; love affairs; harmonious; public relations; sociable; cultured; refined; fashionable.
♀ ♏	Passionate love; secret affairs; sexual magnetism; personal pride; jealous; loves intrigue; transformed by love; destructive passions; intense creativity.
♀ ♐	Many loves; enjoys travelling; foreign friends; cultured; literary; honest in love; open affections; enjoys sport; fun-loving; high-spirited; generous.
♀ ♑	Mature love; undemonstrative; faithful; socially ambitious; appreciates composition and structure; architecture; enjoys work; older friends.
♀ ♒	Sociable; many friends; exciting; unconventional relationships; free love; women's groups; modern art; short-lived relationships; enjoys shocking.
♀ ♓	Loving; soul unions; imaginative; revelling; giving; inspired art; musical; dependent; lazy; seducible; impressionable; romantic; soft-hearted.

MARS

Mars symbolises *desire, aggression, will, activity, impulse, competition, sex* and *sexual drive, initiative, battles, anger* and *masculinity*. It is male sexuality in contradistinction to the feminine sexuality of Venus. In a woman's chart, it often symbolises the ideal male image within the psyche that gives rise to attraction to those who embody or evoke it. It is personified by *assertive men or women, competitors, athletes, mechanics, fire fighters, aggressors, warriors*, etc. In the horoscope, it is the point that reveals the nature of our desires and how we assert ourselves. Its sign, House position and the aspects it makes to other planets show how we get what we want. It also shows the area of life in which we are most energised and aggressive, and how our desires and ability to assert ourselves are integrated with the rest of the psyche.

♂ ♈	Active; aggressive; fighting spirit; competitive; self-willed; dynamic; courageous; shows initiative; angry; tough; assertive; athletic prowess.
♂ ♉	Patient; deliberate; sensual; practical; business skill; salesmanship; strong; obstinate; working with nature; persistent; slow to anger.
♂ ♊	Mobile; mentally assertive; agile; argumentative; hasty; resourceful; heated debates; sarcastic wit; critical; alert; fast cars; decisive.
♂ ♋	Irritable, actively caring; protective; frustrated; passionate; suppressed anger; instinctive actions; moody; active home life; family quarrels.
♂ ♌	Domineering; loud; commanding; winning contests; competitive; egotistical; strong-willed; spirited; acting; leading; bossy; proud.
♂ ♍	Practical or mechanical skills; craftsmanship; critical; physical fitness; exercise; methodical; helpful; medical work; slow to anger.
♂ ♎	Social; charming; smooth; ardent; flirtatious; unassertive; peaceable; enmity; romantic; love affairs; passive; refined; impulsive relationships.
♂ ♏	Strong-willed; intense; powerful sexuality; courageous; resourceful; dominating; grudges; enemies; manipulative; obsessive; survival instinct.
♂ ♐	Frank; noble; blunt; sporty; well-travelled; comradeship; hearty; jovial; adventurous; religious disputes; strong beliefs; dogmatic.
♂ ♑	Ambitious; tough; authoritative; organising; cold; astute; executive ability; hard-working; determined; responsible; business skills.
♂ ♒	Rebellious; cool; self-willed; idealistic; revolutionary; desire for freedom; groups of men; progressive; energetic teamwork; thrill-seeking.
♂ ♓	Romantic; seductive; lacking energy; artistic; resentful; addictive; actively compassionate; dance; energetic on behalf of others; inspired action.

MIDHEAVEN (MC)

The Midheaven (or Xth House cusp) symbolises one's *public image, aspirations, contribution to society, consciousness, aims, direction, future* and *professional life*. It is our public life as distinct from our private life, symbolised by the IC.

Its sign position and aspects to the planets or Ascendant show the nature of our orientation to society (and the public) and how our goals or public life are integrated with rest of our life.

MC ♈	Dynamic, aggressive or pioneering public image; ambitious; confident in public; optimistic; self-assertive; takes initiative; clear aims; establishing individuality.
MC ♉	Patient pursuit of aims; striving for security; aiming for wealth; determined; conservative; productive; stable; career involving art, money or sales; liked by public.
MC ♊	Changing goals; flexible; several careers; writing; teaching; the media; communications skills; intelligent public image; multi-faceted; articulate.
MC ♋	Sensitive to public mood; family aids career; security through work; heritage; caring career/public image; guidance from mother; dedicated.
MC ♌	Self-confident; organising; leadership; creative career; acting; authoritative; admired; egocentric; influential; recognised; determined; sunny public image.
MC ♍	Dedication; service; striving for security; hard-working; high standards; organised; detailed work; impeccable; helping professions; medicine.
MC ♎	Advancement through partnership or co-operation; joint goals; seeks public approval; attractive public image; aims for harmony; social standing.
MC ♏	Passionate pursuit of goals; ambitious; desire for power; persevering; ruthless; hard-working; fanatical aims; demanding work; shrewd; powerful public image.
MC ♐	Optimistic; many goals; aspiring; philosophical or religious aims; recognised; teaching; successful; positive; confident public image.
MC ♑	Ambitious; career-orientated; hard-working; slow but sure advancement; focused; industry; determined; disciplined; prominence; achievement; authoritative; business; seeks status.
MC ♒	Idealistic; scientific or humanitarian goals; rebellious or unusual public image; progressive; unconventional or technological career.
MC ♓	Sensitive public image; unclear goals; unambitious; drifting; social or humanitarian service; unselfish; artistic career; vocation; caring professions; charity.

JUPITER

Jupiter symbolises *expansion, optimism, philosophy, excess, generosity, wisdom, opportunity, growth, religion, learning, aspirations, enthusiasms, indulgence, positivity* and *vision*. It is the opposite of the principle of contraction symbolised by Saturn. It is personified by *successful people, teachers, patrons, adventurers, preachers* and *the wealthy*. It shows what we enjoy in life and how we expand beyond our usual limitations. It offers opportunity and luck, and promotes trust, faith and wisdom, though can also inflate and lead to excess.

The sign, House position and the aspects it makes to other planets indicate what we enjoy, the area of life in which we grow and which naturally presents opportunities and how our ability to relax and enjoy life integrates with the rest of the psyche.

♃ ♈	Leading; popular; pioneering; noble; dynamic; freedom-loving; confident; outgoing; well-known; missionary; heroic; sporting; strong personality; honest; well-travelled.
♃ ♉	Hedonistic; fortunate; business skills; reliable; gluttony; wealthy; generous; abundance; luxury; wasteful; self-indulgent; many possessions; the arts; materialist.
♃ ♊	Confident communicator; informed; well-read; travel; the media; educated; enjoys learning; languages; sociable; restless; scattered; literature; superficial; chatty; good connections.
♃ ♋	Homely; religious; happy family; traditional; attachments; good host; gluttony; real estate; land; caring; charitable; loving; kindly; warm-hearted; smothering; benevolent.
♃ ♌	Extravagant; many loves; excess; entertaining; expansive; fortunate; grandiose; prominent; warm-hearted; honourable; outgoing; theatrical; self-confident; spectacular; creative.
♃ ♍	Organised; ethical; moral; enjoys service; thorough; workaholic; integrity; many jobs; perfectionist; impeccable; planning; medicine; healthy; health interests; physically fit.
♃ ♎	Sociable; popular; just; reasonable; diplomatic; upstanding; well-connected; cultured; good marriage; the law; fashionable; fortunate partnerships; philanthropic; artistic; charitable.

♃ ♏	Highly sexed; love of power; shrewd; seeks wealth; metaphysics; love of mystery; investigative; self-discovery; good psychologist; confessional; insightful; explores taboos.
♃ ♐	Teaching; love of learning; well-travelled; literary; philosophical; adventurous; expansive; confident; wise; preaching; optimistic; seeks freedom; foreign contacts; belief; faith; religion.
♃ ♑	Prominent; responsible; workaholic; integrity; recognised; capable; seeks status; conservative; restrained; trusted; tight; good connections; ambitious; earned success.
♃ ♒	Many friends; popular; fellowship; idealistic; liberal; radical; visionary; original; reforming; unorthodox; inventive; campaigning; humanitarian.
♃ ♓	Rich inner life; compassionate; charitable; caring; relaxed; indolent; altruistic; imaginative; visionary; addictive; love of solitude; spiritual; healing; trust in the cosmos.

SATURN

Saturn symbolises *restriction, limitations, duty, work, crystallisation, concentration, inhibition, discipline, focus, form* and *wisdom*. It is the principle of contraction unlike the expansion represented by Jupiter. It is personified by the *elderly, business people, depressives, pessimists, authority figures, law enforcers, workers* and *judges*.

In the horoscope it is the point that reveals the nature of the limitations (either within or without) that we must face and work with in our lives. Its sign, House position and the aspects it makes to other planets show the nature of our limitations, the area of life in which we are tested and how our capacity for taking responsibility is integrated with the rest of the psyche.

| ♄ ♈ | Independent; strong character; self-reliant; inhibited; lonely; defiant; esteemed; self-disciplined; responsible; strong-willed; serious; focused. |
| ♄ ♉ | Trustworthy; strong values; materialistic; grasping; stable; fear of poverty; hard-working; determined; slow to adapt; patient; seeks security. |

♄ ♊	Serious-minded; slow learner; study; logical; intellectually defensive; critical; fear of criticism or appearing stupid; thoughtful; speech problems; profound, thorough.
♄ ♋	Inner strength; seeks emotional security; fear of rejection; coldness at home; sheltering; integrity; defensive; reclusive; emotional maturity; deep feelings.
♄ ♌	Seeks respect; unspontaneous; aloof; creative inhibitions; authoritarian; serious love; dignified; impressive performance; difficulties with children.
♄ ♍	Hard-working; self-critical; health problems; fear of chaos; nit-picking; craftsmanship; practical skills; serving others; hypochondria; anxious; worrying; perfectionist.
♄ ♎	Fidelity; public duties; serious or older partner; conventional; commitment to relationships; faithful; the law; justice; fear of rejection; serious-minded.
♄ ♏	Strong-willed; seeks control; hidden depths; shrewd; melancholy; profound; tough; survival instinct; financial affairs; metaphysics; secrets; fear of letting go.
♄ ♐	Honourable; ethical; orthodox religion; the law; knowledge; limited horizons; practical idealism; sermonising; sceptical; principled; pessimistic; self-righteous; judgmental; learned.
♄ ♑	Responsible; goal-conscious; hard-working; slow but sure advancement; strict; late starter; traditional; repressed; fear of failure; conservative; patient; disciplined; organised; respected.
♄ ♒	Unconventional; actively humanitarian; uncomfortable in groups; false friends; detached; abstract; scientific; an outsider; loner; friendships important; dedication to ideals.
♄ ♓	Spiritual or psychological struggles; hidden depths; withdrawal; self-sacrificial; reclusive; shy; introspective; contemplative; charitable work.

The Moon's North Node

The North Node of the Moon (Dragon's Head) symbolises *growth, development, individuality, potential, karma, the future, providence, meaning* and *The Path*. The South Node (Dragon's Tail) (which is always directly opposite the North Node) symbolises *the path of least resistance, stagnation, the past, repetition, habit* and *loss of self*. We need to learn to balance the urges represented by the Moon's Nodes,

overcoming the pull towards habit and the past symbolised by the South Node, whilst using the lessons learned from it to help develop the potentials symbolised by the North Node. By doing so we experience the joy of inner fulfilment and the certainty that we are treading our destined path in life. In the horoscope the North Node's sign, House position and the aspects it makes to other planets indicate our potential, the area of life in which we are called to grow and fulfil our destiny, and how our path to fulfilment integrates with the rest of our lives.

☊ ♈	Growth through self-assertion; undermining relationships *vs.* independence; loss of self *vs.* self-discovery; following *vs.* leading; other people's expectations *vs.* one's own.
☊ ♉	Growth through practical achievement; talent for business or art; self-worth *vs.* worth to others; emotional complexities; sexual pleasure *vs.* sexual power; creating abundance.
☊ ♊	Growth through using one's intelligence; talent for communication and expression of ideas; writing; dislike of being tied down; wandering; restless; perpetual student.
☊ ♋	Growth through caring or parenthood; nourishment; overemphasis on status, success, or respect; dislike of admitting failure; capacity to love; emotional fulfilment.
☊ ♌	Growth through leadership or love; 'fitting in' *vs.* acceptance of individuality; intellect frustrates need for love; creative fulfilment.
☊ ♍	Growth through work or self-mastery; escapist; excessive daydreaming; development of practical skills and discrimination; physical health *vs.* fantasy life.
☊ ♎	Growth through relationships; creative partnership; overly self-reliant; teamwork; development of social awareness; culture.
☊ ♏	Growth through insight; sexual fulfilment; overemphasis on money or material values; development of the will; insight; conservative; rebirth.
☊ ♐	Growth through learning or travel; broadening the mind; teaching; vacillating; chatter; superficial; quest for knowledge.
☊ ♑	Growth through achievement; contribution to society; dependence *vs.* independence; fear of success; sentimental attachments; growth into maturity; recognised; career fulfilment.

| ♌ ♒ | Growth through friendship; development of individuality; impersonal or scientific interests; research; humanitarian causes; egotism; role-playing. |
| ♌ ♓ | Growth through spirituality or imagination; the way of the heart; over-analytical; self-critical; growth of compassion; material concerns *vs.* spiritual growth. |

URANUS

Uranus symbolises *shock, change, independence, the new, invention, rebellion, individuality, excitement, originality, inspiration, unorthodoxy* and *reform*. It is personified by *technicians, rebels, aliens, individuals, eccentrics, crazy people, revolutionaries, reformers,* and those who are unusual or different in some way. It is the principle of freedom and the breaking away from the rigid structures that Saturn represents. In the horoscope Uranus reveals how we express our uniqueness and individuality. Its sign, House position and the aspects it makes to other planets show where we differ from the norm, the area of life in which we have to be free to go our own way and how our desire for freedom is integrated with the rest of the psyche.

Uranus is the first of the three outer planets (along with Neptune and Pluto), whose effects are less noticeable in the individual than in the collective, unless we are particularly attuned to it by way of aspects of the inner planets or to the Ascendant.

♅ ♈	Headstrong; pioneering; individual; idealistic; utopian; rebellious; unconventional; self-willed; restless; daring; erratic; reforming; abrupt; tactless; adventurous; quick; active.
♅ ♉	Resourceful; entrepreneurial; strong-willed; fluctuating finances; speculation; wheeler dealing; electronic commerce; risk-taking; economic reforms; ingenious; modern art.
♅ ♊	Original ideas; abstract; questioning; fast cars; sharp; witty; bizarre interests; quick mind; intuitive understanding; science; information technology; intellectual.
♅ ♋	Rebellion against parental tradition; progressive or unusual home life; communal living; restless; insecure; changes of residence; erratic; volatile; inner freedom.

♅ ♌	Individualistic; egomaniac; free love; strong-willed; headstrong; exciting; determined; creative originality; artistic freedom; dramatic; shocking; unusual love affairs; prodigies.
♅ ♍	Inventive; technological or mechanical skills; ingenious; intellectual; critical; brilliant; computers; unusual employment; unconventional methods; erratic health; holistic health.
♅ ♎	Social reform; sudden attachments; unconventional or short-lived relationships; free love; new social patterns; magnetic; artistic; stylish; trend-setting; uncommitted; hedonistic.
♅ ♏	Strong-willed; transformative; sexually liberated; taboo breaking; courageous; danger-loving; compulsive; explosive; volatile; psychological insight; extremist.
♅ ♐	Libertarian; unorthodox beliefs; adventurous; rebellious; free-spirited; progressive education; utopian; prophetic; foreign adventures; restless; broad-minded; gambling.
♅ ♑	Free enterprise; the marketplace; breaking with tradition; initiative; unusual career; volatile business; radical aims; anti-establishment; structural reforms.
♅ ♒	Inventive; progressive; utopian; rebellious; social reform; seeks change; new technology; shared ideals; mass movements; unusual groups; free thinking; democratic.
♅ ♓	Intuitive; visionary; ecstasy; unusual experiences; mysticism; the occult; unrealistic; strange complexes; crazy wisdom; inspired lunacy; parapsychology; inner liberation.

NEPTUNE

Neptune symbolises *spirituality, diffusion, merging, compassion, imagination, transcendence, inspiration, universality, illusion and disillusion, dreams, ESP, drugs, hallucinations, the occult, self-sacrifice, the unconscious and the collective unconscious, myth, bliss, psychosis, weakness* and *delusion*. It is personified by *mystics, dreamers, addicts* and *martyrs*. It represents loss, transcendence or escape from one's time-bound and finite ego and absorption in something vaster and more unbounded. Neptune is the second of the three outer planets. Its sign, House position and the aspects it makes to other planets, show what our generation is particularly

sensitive to and how our capacity to lose boundaries is integrated with the rest of the psyche.

♆ ♈	Sensitive; confused; lethargic; unselfish; aimless; spiritual pioneers; idealistic bravery; determination to implement vision.
♆ ♉	Idealisation of nature; sharing resources; confusion over territory; simple living; spiritual materialism; aesthetic appreciation; art.
♆ ♊	Idealistic; inspired thinking; poetry; sensitive-minded; confusion; impressionable; sensitive literature; imaginative.
♆ ♋	Nostalgic; idealisation of home and family; cherishing; inner richness; emotionally sensitive; nursing; love of homeland.
♆ ♌	Acting; theatre; cinema; mystique; romanic; hedonistic; pretence; open-hearted; art; idealism in love; extravagant; sensitive children; self-deluded; speculation; gambling; playful.
♆ ♍	Reflective; gentle; thoughtful; good manners; helpful; selfless service; nutrition; holistic health; hypochondria; fastidious; healing abilities; disorganised; delicate; confusion at work.
♆ ♎	Humanitarian; idealistic; 'peace and love'; romanticism; seeks social harmony; idealised or confused relationships; utopian; love of the arts; flower power.
♆ ♏	Secretive; soulful; spiritual transformations; mysterious; hidden power; the occult; the unconscious mind; parapsychology; sexual confusion; profound; psychotherapy.
♆ ♐	Spiritual beliefs; exploration; prophetic; literary; idealistic; gurus; search for God; long journeys; confusion abroad; religious freedom; false prophets; tolerant; utopian.
♆ ♑	Glamorisation of work; dissolving outdated structures; unambitious; designer living; style as content; world government; practical spirituality; relief of suffering.
♆ ♒	Futuristic visions; glamorisation of science; social idealism; humanitarian aspirations; mass movements; acceptance of diversity; cultural renewal; utopianism.
♆ ♓	Compassion; religious renewal; mysticism; spiritual growth; tolerance; peace; mass confusion; spiritual phenomena; illusions.

PLUTO

Pluto symbolises *the orgasm, death, transformation, destruction, rebirth, power, evolution, the masses, regeneration, revolution, underworld, war, atomic power, biology, survival,* and *conception.* It is personified by *dictators, revolutionaries* and *influencers,* and represents the process of destruction of old forms and the release of the energy inherent in them in order to create new life. Pluto is the third and last of the outer planets. It sign, House position and the aspects it makes to other planets show our generation's primary orientation to life, the area of life in which we are likely to experience major transformations and how our power and will integrate with the rest of the psyche.

♇ ♈	Powerful personalities; volcanic; dictatorship; fascination; destruction; creation of a new order; pioneering.
♇ ♉	Economic power; conflict over land or territory; transformation of commerce; insatiable; consuming; lust; self-preservation.
♇ ♊	Transformed means of communication; powerful intellects; mass persuasion; mental manipulation; death of old ideas.
♇ ♋	Emotional power; protective instincts; national survival; pulling together; family power struggles; motherland; destruction of nuclear family; patriotic; disruption of roots.
♇ ♌	Youth revolution; will to power; rock and roll; loud; rebellious; creative power; sexual and artistic revolution; life as play.
♇ ♍	Hypercritical; incisive; acerbic; profound; mass of detail; profound research; health revolution; mass unemployment; change in work practices.
♇ ♎	Transformation of society; fated partnerships; intense attractions; fame; divorce; breakdown of relationships; anti-social; revolutionary.
♇ ♏	Personal transformation; life-and-death issues; survival; destruction; deep changes; regeneration; economic reform; darkness; instinct; sexual power.
♇ ♐	Destruction of old beliefs; fundamentalism; dogma; power of truth; bigotry; new forms of travel; propaganda; transformation of religion.
♇ ♑	Destruction of outworn structures; governmental breakdown; transformation of business; anti-establishment; economic reform; extreme ambition.

45

| ♀ ≈ | Social breakdown; subversion; anarchy; revolution; political transformation; reformist; mass movements; collective power. |
| ♀ ✕ | Spiritual transformation; apocalypyic; profound; destruction of old myths; the collective unconscious; metaphysics; supernatural experiences. |

The Houses of the horoscope

As mentioned in Chapter 2, the twelve Houses represent different **areas of life experience**. Whereas the planets symbolise the different functions within our own psyche, the Houses show us in what area of our lives those functions tend to manifest. The VIth House, for instance, represents work and health. If we have Venus in the VIth House, we are likely to enjoy our work, make friends easily with work colleagues and perhaps employ artistic or social skills in our work. We are also likely to enjoy keeping ourselves fit and healthy, perhaps through exercise and by paying attention to the quality of the food we eat.

In a birthchart, Houses containing several planets symbolise important areas of the person's life. For instance, two or three planets in the Xth House indicate someone for whom work or a career is particularly important.

The meaning of the twelve Houses relates to (although is not the same as) the meaning of the twelve signs.

The table opposite gives keywords for each house, together with the sign it relates to.

House	Life area	House mode	Related sign
I	Body type, personality, appearance	Angular	Aries
II	Financial resources, sources of money, possessions, values	Succedent	Taurus
III	Siblings, neighbours, mind, junior education	Cadent	Gemini
IV	Home, family, background, emotional resources	Angular	Cancer
V	Creativity, children, love affairs, self-expression	Succedent	Leo
VI	Work, health, daily routine, secondary education	Cadent	Virgo
VII	Partnership, marriage partner, relationships	Angular	Libra
VIII	Sex, jointly owned possessions, the psyche	Succedent	Scorpio
IX	Beliefs, philosophy of life, higher education	Cadent	Sagittarius
X	Career, goals, social status	Angular	Capricorn
XI	Friendships, groups, society, ideals	Succedent	Aquarius
XII	The unconscious, inner world, spirituality	Cadent	Pisces

House modes

The twelve Houses are divided into those that are Angular, Succedent or Cadent. Angular Houses (I, IV, VII and X) are traditionally regarded as strengthening in their influence on the planets they contain, whilst Succedent Houses (II, V, VIII and XI) are regarded as neutral. Cadent Houses (III, VI, IX and XII) are regarded as weakening in their effect.

However, it is more useful to regard the Angular Houses are relating to sources of *identity* (appearance, family life, marriage and career), the Succedent Houses as sources of *satisfaction and security* (money, love, sex and friendship) and the Cadent Houses as sources of *learning* (communication, skills, beliefs and spirituality).

House rulers

The cusp of each house is naturally in a sign. The planet ruling that sign is said to be the *House ruler*. For instance, if Scorpio is on the cusp of the IVth House, the ruler of the IVth House is thus Mars (or Pluto). House rulers give additional information about the area of life the House governs, which is particularly useful if the House is untenanted, i.e. has no planets within it. For a fuller discussion, see *Planets in Houses* by Robert Pelletier, or *The Twelve Houses* by Howard Sasportas (see Appendix 2).

Planets in Houses

Following are tables giving keywords for planets in each House.

SUN IN THE HOUSES

☉ I	Personality; strong will; vitality; radiance; lively; seeks attention; arrogant; confident; brave; self-centred; noble; leadership; energy; egocentric.
☉ II	Secure; enjoyment of life; sensual; sex; financial and material confidence; strong values; making money; acquisitive; earning power; financial independence; ownership; self-worth.
☉ III	Articulate; fluent; witty; writing skills; sociable; observant; quick; intelligent; dextrous; versatile; communication skills; mental and verbal skills; mobile.
☉ IV	Caring, secure; private; shelter; traditional; roots; family life important; parenthood; childhood; creation of a happy home; leadership at home.
☉ V	Self-expressive; leading; domineering; artistic; love affairs; fun-loving; entertaining; creative; attention-seeking; likes children; personality.
☉ VI	Skilled; seeks service; hard-working; dedicated; practical; methodical; technical; good health; fitness; seeks leading role in work; organised; creative work.

☉ VII	Seeks partnership; enjoys relating; contact with the public; the law; popular; harmonious; sociable; dislike of solitude; takes lead in relationships; discovers self through others.
☉ VIII	Intense; secretive; intimate; controls other people's resources; seeks regeneration or transformation; breaks taboos; sexual; interest in the afterlife or the occult; passion.
☉ IX	Higher education; travel; learning; seeking; religion; teaching; foreign contacts; creative philosophy of life; seeks freedom; broad-minded; tolerant; belief; intellectual leadership.
☉ X	Ambitious; successful; career important; authority; seeks recognition; perseverance; dedication; hard-working; responsible; goal-orientated; executive or managerial ability.
☉ XI	Humanitarian; collective; group-orientated; friendship; idealistic; scientific; unorthodox; utopian; liberal; political; modern; experimental.
☉ XII	Compassionate; self-sacrificing; behind-the-scenes creativity; spiritual leadership; hidden; institutions; reflective; healing; illumination.

MOON IN THE HOUSES

☽ I	Sensitive or caring personality; changeable; emotional; displays of feeling; strong responses; parental; moody; subjective; irritable; domestic life and parenthood important.
☽ II	Needs material security; stable family life; comfort; financial instincts; self-preservation; habit; possessions; heirlooms and antiques; attachment to places, property, things.
☽ III	Sensitive communicator; care of siblings; close contacts; subjective thought and speech; good memory; changing ideas; gossip; advice; counselling; friendly; personal involvement.
☽ IV	Needs emotional security; rich home life; family ties; parenthood; cherishing; nurturing; love of mother; smothered; caring; habitual; domestic; stable; the past; childhood important.
☽ V	Sensitive or instinctive creativity; needs love; popular; ardent; romantic; artistic; needs drama; vain; cares for children; expressive; entertaining; joyful; seeks attention.
☽ VI	Needs work; dedicated; psychosomatic illnesses; daily routine gives security; practical care of others; nursing; busy; sensitive to criticism.

☽ VII	Close partnerships; sensitive partner; dependent relationships; mother's partner; sharing; supportive; personal contact; inconstant; needs harmony; co-operative.
☽ VIII	Deep feelings; security through sex; needs intimacy; sensitive to undercurrents; introspective; psychological understanding; hidden depths; possessive; deep attachments.
☽ IX	Simple faith; need for freedom; emotional honesty; frankness; inherited beliefs; limited horizons; love of travel; home abroad; religious feelings; changeable beliefs; restless.
☽ X	Caring career; need to succeed; sensitive public image; emotional fulfilment through work; career women; career and family links; support network.
☽ XI	Concern for others; caring friends; group sharing; community; public spirit; joining; support groups; emotional friendships; shared hopes; needs to belong; family of friends.
☽ XII	Self-sacrificial; needs peace; mediumistic; susceptible; compassionate; sensitive to suffering; healing; charity; needs to strengthen boundaries; reflective; spiritual nourishment.

MERCURY IN THE HOUSES

☿ I	Talkative; humorous; lively; youthful; active mind; precocious; noisy; alert; speaking and writing; mobile; well-travelled; witty; flexible; bright.
☿ II	Business sense; financial dealings; skilled negotiator; collects books; clear values; practical mentality; fixed opinions; resourceful; changeable finances.
☿ III	Articulate; witty; fluent; languages; enjoys learning; siblings; neighbours; discussion; mobile; transport; writing skills; well-read; informed; observant.
☿ IV	Busy home-life; talking about feelings; reading encouraged in childhood; inherited ideas; intelligent or clever parents; changes of residence; good communication with family.
☿ V	Creative mentality; mental games; contests; fun; creative writing; good storyteller; jokes; good communication with children; teaching children; enjoys learning; entertaining.
☿ VI	Job involves communication or information; commuting; sociable colleagues; busy work; orderly; specialised skills; methodical; logical; accurate; criticism; collating.

☿ VII	Communication with public; mediation; counselling; advising; diplomacy; teamwork; co-operative; public-minded; sociable; youthful or intelligent partner; intellectual partnership.
☿ VIII	Penetrating intellect; interest in occult, psychology, sex or afterlife; fascinating; detection; investigative; analytical; researching; exploring taboos; love of mysteries.
☿ IX	Higher education; learning; teaching; travel; foreign contacts; ethical; scattered; open; debate; philosophy; religion; publishing; writing; idealistic; restless; exploratory.
☿ X	Communications industry; career involves travel; teaching; writing; planning; lecturing; administration; the media; training; public speaking; public relations; organised; clear goals.
☿ XI	Democratic; sharing ideas in groups; spokesperson; politics; progressive ideas; detached or scientific mentality; young friends; teams; societies or clubs; social activity; reform; joining.
☿ XII	Poetic; lyrical; mediumistic; imaginative; intuitive; images; reflective; inspired; confused; the unconscious mind; non-verbal communication; contemplative; neurotic; introspective.

VENUS IN THE HOUSES

♀ I	Attractive personality; beautiful; graceful; popular; stylish; fashionable; active social life; charming; courteous; artistic; seductive; beautiful environment; cultured; indulgent.
♀ II	Attracts money; beautiful possessions; good taste; hedonistic; love of luxury; self-indulgent; gourmet; erotica; enjoys security; sensual; greedy; love of nature; artistic work.
♀ III	Friendly; good humoured; eloquent; writing; lyrical; love of words; literature; poetry; neighbourly; likes siblings; sisters; pleasant speech; enjoyed early school; school friends.
♀ IV	Happy home life; warm; familial; comfortable; sentimental; good host; enjoys caring for others; parents as friends; attractive or stylish home; fun in childhood; art encouraged early.
♀ V	Love affairs; pleasurable self-expression; creative; love of art and drama; theatre; romantic; ardent; entertainment; fun; good with children.

♀ VI	Enjoys work; artistic work; design; good relationship with co-workers; connoisseur; crafts; attractive work environment; whole food; health/beauty/fitness programmes; good health.
♀ VII	Happy marriage; romance; love; charming; refined; cultured; sociable; liked; attractive or artistic partner; diplomatic; peacemaking; seeks public approval.
♀ VIII	Sexually artful; sex as fun; alluring; love of mysteries; financial gain through partner; soul-love; sharing resources; inheritance.
♀ IX	Love of travel; foreign friends and contacts; philosophical; enjoys religion; happy holidays; exploring; enjoys learning; bonhomie; teaching; well-read.
♀ X	Love of career, successful, social ambition; artistic career; harmonious work environment; friends in high places; cultivating good contacts; cosmetic or fashion industry.
♀ XI	Friendly, sociable; group-orientated; sharing; women's groups; artistic friends; female friends; hip; fashionable; the 'in' crowd; friends as lovers.
♀ XII	Inspired art; compassionate; loving; love of solitude; giving; escapist; longing; legends; music; poetry; art galleries, museums, etc.; secret relationships; hidden talents; imaginative.

CARS IN ThE houSES

♂ I	Assertive personality; dynamic; fit; tough or macho image; strong; impatient; lively; temper; courageous; competitive; sexual; restless; sport; initiative; stamina; independence; athletic.
♂ II	Entertaining; seeks wealth; business skills; obstinate; impulse buying; territorial; impatient; defends values; proselytising; hard work; sexually assertive; building.
♂ III	Mental energy; quick-thinking; stimulating; argumentative; critical; forceful speaking or writing; direct; repartee; challenging; aggressive sibling(s); mobile; fast cars; disagreements.
♂ IV	Protective instincts; passionate; hidden anger; intense feelings; moody; assertive family; difficulties with parents; active home life; head of the household; defends loved ones.

♂ V	Creative energy; passionate creativity; ardent; egotistical; pursuit of love; acting; competitive sports; contests; bossy; spirited; tough or independent children; daring; seeks attention.
♂ VI	Hard-working; mastery; efficient; aggressive co-workers or employees; challenging work; male colleagues; machines; anger affects health; energetic exercises; vibrant; fit.
♂ VII	Passionate or impulsive relationships; argumentative; teamwork; unco-operative; enemies; marital conflict; ardour; hard-working partnerships; disagreements; competitive.
♂ VIII	Powerful sexuality; forceful; strong-willed; passionate; intense; violent; survival instinct; secret activities; seeks power; battles over joint finances; legacies, etc.; lust; persistent.
♂ IX	Much-travelled; blunt; outspoken; sporting; enthusiastic; contests; religious or philosophical disputes; adventures; difficulties; rude; dogmatic; angry God; foreign men.
♂ X	Ambitious; competitive; executive ability; industry; hard-working; determined; organised; desire for power; tough work; achievement; initiative; enterprising; conflict with boss.
♂ XI	Defends freedom; independent; reforming; rebellious; male friends; active or aggressive groups; active participation; political; disagreements amongst friends; crusading; teamwork.
♂ XII	Spiritual leadership; behind-the-scenes activity; energetic on behalf of others; charitable work; artistic energy; secret passions; repressed anger; primal scream; wounded.

JUPITER IN THE HOUSES

♃ I	Confident personality; generous; loud; noble; fortunate; self-important; excessive; corpulent; travel; philosophical; wealthy; optimistic; aspiring; sporting; adventurous.
♃ II	Abundance; generous; wealth; over-indulgence; jovial; sexy; hedonistic; comfortable; business skills; self-worth; profit; ostentatious; luxury; wasteful; appetite; opulence.

♃ III	Sociable; many contacts; mobile; travel; enjoys learning; teaching; widely read; the media; publishing; questioning; bright; fortunate siblings; lecturing; writing; languages; chatter.
♃ IV	Happy home life; hospitable; kind; religious; many homes; real estate; comfortable; learning at home; secure; congenial; good ancestry; inherited wisdom; large or opulent home.
♃ V	Many loves; self-confident; dignified; creative; proud; many or fortunate children; winning; ostentatious; lucky in love; gambling; inflated ego; games; acting; theatrical; dramatic.
♃ VI	Enjoys work; popular at work; loves order; healthy; fitness; exercise; healing; ethical; workaholic; high standards; honourable service; medicine; multi-skilled; self-improvement.
♃ VII	Happy marriage; wealthy or foreign partner; just; popular; fashionable; good connections; socially gifted; flattery; unpossessive; growth through partnership; learns through others.
♃ VIII	Psychological growth; sexual excess; legacies; love of mystery; stewardship; fortunate investment; the occult; peaceful death; discovery of faith; love of power; healthy finances.
♃ IX	Well-travelled; educated; philosophical; liberal; philanthropic; principled; expansive; humorous; the law; teaching; literature; broadcasting; values truth; cultured; religious.
♃ X	Successful career; prominent; recognised; famous; seeks status; professional; reliable; good standing; overbearing; executive or managerial flair; business skills; freedom through work.
♃ XI	Many or successful friends; sociable; humanitarian; shared aspirations; many hopes and wishes; friendly; liberal; patronage; idealistic groups; benevolent.
♃ XII	Compassionate; imaginative; charitable; visionary; relaxed; love of solitude; rich inner life; addictive; prophetic dreams; spiritual teaching; gurus; guidance; peace; music and art.

SATURN IN THE HOUSES

♄ I	Serious personality; professional front; reserved; ambitious; sober; formal; introspective; mature; self-disciplined; self-critical; insecure; late starter; achievement; bony; gaunt.
♄ II	Fear of poverty; hard-working; persevering; economical; acquisitive; tenacious; shrewd; frugal; determined; lack of self-worth; traditional values; financial acumen; sexual anxieties.
♄ III	Serious mentality; intellectual; quiet; studious; communication difficulties; problems with siblings; logical; concentration; critical; thorough; introspective; slow learner.
♄ IV	Difficult family life; inner strength; integrity; deep feelings; surface coldness; family duties; work at home; strict upbringing; reclusive; search for roots; land; fear of closeness.
♄ V	Unconfident; creative blocks; difficulties with children; older or serious lovers; unspontaneous; loyal; serious; art; self-conscious; desire for respect; fear of rejection.
♄ VI	Hard-working; meticulous; service; practical skills; methodical; administration; labouring; exploitation; anxiety; stress; hypochondria; difficulties with employers, co-workers, etc.
♄ VII	Older partner; late marriage; fidelity; public duty; estrangements; justice; the law; enemies; fear of rejection; marital problems; unequal partnerships; working at relationships.
♄ VIII	Fear of letting go; controlling; melancholy; inner strength; shrewd; introspective; the occult; difficulties with inheritances or shared finances; prudent; sexual inhibitions; guilt feelings.
♄ IX	Stoical; religious duties; limited horizons; self-educated; ethical problems; importance of truth; respectable; difficulties abroad; harsh or traditional religion; deep thinking.
♄ X	Ambitious; workaholic; clear goals; focused; patient; earned success; egocentric; dictatorial; fear of authority; lonely; authoritative; difficulties with parents; achievement; honour.
♄ XI	Older friends; social inhibitions; alienation; isolated; dislike of groups; hard-working groups; an outsider; committed to ideals; false friends; humanitarian work.
♄ XII	Work in seclusion; hidden fears; buried hurts; guilt; fear of the irrational or confinement; nursing; spiritual strength; service; spiritual work; solace; caring institutions.

The Moon's North Node in the Houses

☊ I	Growth through leadership; development of the personality; independence *vs.* dependence; self-fulfilment *vs.* conformity to others' expectations.
☊ II	Growth through material success; personal worth *vs.* worth to others; tangible achievements *vs.* search for power; growth through work, development of self-worth.
☊ III	Growth through communication; restless; guru façade; development of intellect; empty teaching; talent for writing or speaking.
☊ IV	Growth through caring; emotional fulfilment *vs.* public status or career success; home *vs.* work; talent for nurturing; joyful parenthood; inner riches; empty achievement.
☊ V	Growth through leadership or creativity; empty socialising; alienation; fulfilment through love; expressing self *vs.* 'fitting in'.
☊ VI	Growth through development of skills, work fulfilment; physical health *vs.* spiritual health; empty spirituality; paranoia *vs.* practicality; healthful living; fruitful; craftsmanship.
☊ VII	Growth through partnership; empty self-reliance; over-concern with self or image; co-operation *vs.* independence; talent for relating; fulfilment in love.
☊ VIII	Growth through inner transformation; materialism *vs.* psychological growth; development of willpower; empty materialism; lust *vs.* intimacy; rebirth; facing one's demons.
☊ IX	Growth through learning; fulfilment through teaching; tourism *vs.* discovering other cultures; empty words; doubt *vs.* faith; knowledge *vs.* wisdom.
☊ X	Growth through achievement; security *vs.* public success; family duties *vs.* pursuit of goals; fulfilment through work or career; stagnation.
☊ XI	Growth through friendship; love affairs *vs.* pursuit of ideals; fulfilment through pursuit of social or humanitarian causes; empty creativity; dependent on praise.
☊ XII	Growth through spirituality; empty routine; criticism of self and others; overly rational; hidden talents; fulfilment through inner exploration; development of rich inner life.

URANUS IN THE HOUSES

♅ I	Original personality; exciting; dynamic; eccentric; self-willed; highly strung; unconventional; headstrong; creative; catalytic; rebellious; progressive; unusual appearance; shocking.
♅ II	Entrepreneurial; financial upheavals; speculation; sudden windfalls; unusual possessions; whiz kid; electronic trading; unusual work; inventive; eclectic; unorthodox values.
♅ III	Quick mind; brilliant; nervous; rapid speech; misunderstood; radical ideas; precocious; unusual siblings; progressive learning methods; lateral thinking; ingenious; computers.
♅ IV	Unusual home or family; unsettled childhood; emotionally independent; rebellious; upsets; unconventional upbringing; communal living; many homes; progressive child-rearing.
♅ V	Original creativity; headstrong; individualistic; egomaniacal; dramatic; speculation; arty; unpredictable lovers; short-lived affairs; leading; bohemian; unusual children.
♅ VI	Original working methods; erratic employment; self-employment; computers; research; alternative medicine; weird pets; scientific or technical skills; entrepreneurial.
♅ VII	Unorthodox relationships; sudden attachments; free love; social reform; non-committal; unusual partner; marital tensions; exciting social life; catalytic; redefining social roles.
♅ VIII	Strong will; taboo breaking; sexual liberation; unconventional sex; uninhibited; erratic sex-drive; inner transformations; sudden inheritances; psychology; investigative.
♅ IX	Free-thinking; unusual beliefs; utopian; progressive philosophy; adventurous; exciting journeys; prophetic; science fiction; free speech; liberal; exotic cults; esoteric; broadcasting.
♅ X	Technological career; enterprising; sudden success; freedom at work; erratic or chequered career; dislike of tradition or authority; upsetting the status quo; self-motivated.
♅ XI	Progressive ideas; modern; rebellious; unconventional friends; independent; communal; reforming; scientific; inventive; campaigning groups; radical; utopian; free.
♅ XII	Unusual fantasises; visionary; ecstasy; unconscious rebellion; intuitive; synchronicities; insights; revelations; exploration of the unconscious; unusual institutions; complexes.

NEPTUNE IN THE HOUSES

Ψ I	Sensitive personality; glamorous; magnetic; visionary; unselfish; artistic; weak; inspired; impressionable; confused; spiritual; compassionate; sensitive physique; enigmatic; martyred.
Ψ II	Impractical; love of beauty; artistic; speculative; muddles finances; charity; wasteful; spiritual values; sexually vulnerable; sharing; spiritual materialism; glossy images; lazy.
Ψ III	Intuitive; imaginative; poor memory; poetic; whimsical; vague; deceit; sensitive siblings; woolly thinking; inspired; irrational; fiction; literature; spiritual ideas.
Ψ IV	Sensitive; magical or confused childhood; kind; vulnerable; compassionate; sheltered; self-sacrificial; chaotic or artistic family; neuroses; escapist; idealised parents; inner peace.
Ψ V	Romantic; platonic or spiritual love; inspired creativity; artistic; theatre; films; drama; acting; role-play; sensitive children; easily seduced; exaggeration; gambling; self-realisation.
Ψ VI	Service; spiritual healing; confused working methods; humble; gentle; sympathetic; discreet; physical sensitivity; psychosomatic disorders; hypochondriac; medicine; caring work.
Ψ VII	Idealistic relationships; sensitive or artistic partner; romantic; seductive; easily attracted; loving; soul unions; aesthetic; easily misled; counselling; saviour–victim relationships.
Ψ VIII	Inner transformation; spiritual power; secretive; the occult; confused sexuality; erotic fantasies; seducible; mythology; dissipation; financial complications; psychic.
Ψ IX	Truth seeking; prophetic; visionary; long journeys; disillusionment; religion; spiritual teachings; gurus; exotic religions; cults; faith; expanded consciousness; literary; doubt.
Ψ X	Vocation; artistic or caring career; unambitious; unrealistic goals; fear of failure; sensitive to public mood; glamour; unrecognised; loved by public; scandal; dislike of limelight.
Ψ XI	Idealistic friendships; artistic or spiritual groups; social idealism; utopian; unreliable friends; humanitarian causes; secret societies; unsavoury associations; bohemian; sub-cultures.
Ψ XII	Compassionate; vivid dreams; meditation; escapist; empathetic; psychic sensitivity; spiritual; chaotic; martyred; addictive; imaginative; delusions; magic; inner peace; the soul; God.

PLUTO IN THE HOUSES

♇ I	Powerful personality; presence; great energy; transformative; strong-willed; rage; intense; leading; primitive; ruthless; extreme; mysterious; fascinating; enigmatic; compulsive.
♇ II	Financial or economic power; acquisitive; materialistic; great gains and loses; greedy; territorial; proving one's worth; investment; self-made success; lust; insatiable; stubborn.
♇ III	Penetrating intellect; secretive; analytical; difficulties with siblings or early school; influential ideas; incisive; investigative; obsessive; problem solving; cynical; advertising; hypnosis.
♇ IV	Powerful family; heredity; encounter with the past; emotional depth; psychological transformation; solitary; difficult childhood; survival instinct; family secrets; profound.
♇ V	Creative power; intense self-expression; dramatic; dominating; speculative; passionate affairs; difficulties with children; dangerous games; competitive; arrogant; seeks attention.
♇ VI	Demanding or dangerous work; research; dedicated; regeneration; problem solving; health crises; workaholic; great effort; medicine; industry; environmentalism; self-help.
♇ VII	Fated relationships; demanding partner; fascinating; social power; anti-social; celebrated; fanatical attraction; enemies; confrontations; encounters; deep unions.
♇ VIII	Powerful will; survival; transformative; destructive; inner strength; rage; sexual power; compulsive; fated; insightful; power struggles; intrigue; manipulative; hidden depths.
♇ IX	Search for truth; fundamentalist; atheist; difficulties abroad; intolerant; propaganda; nihilist; conflict with teachers; strong opinions; salvation/damnation; zealous; spiritual leadership.
♇ X	Powerful ambition; desire for power or fame; demanding career; achievement; mission; driven; heavy responsibilities; dictatorial; notorious; influential; business skill; control.
♇ XI	Powerful friendships; politically active; rebellious; revolutionary; deep friendships; social catalyst; reforming; subversive groups; causes; progressive; ideological struggle.
♇ XII	Inner transformations; introspective; compulsions; complexes; eruptions; revelations; psychotherapy; the collective unconscious; hidden depths; profound; spiritual power.

Aspects between planets

The aspects show how the planets in a particular horoscope inter-relate. They show the relationships between the psychological functions as symbolised by the planets and can be regarded as either *flowing* or *dynamic*. Flowing aspects (sextiles, trines and some conjunctions) produce an easy interchange of energies and, hence, often represent natural skills and talents that we find easy to draw on. Dynamic aspects (squares, oppositions and some conjunctions) on the other hand produce a certain amount of conflict or stress which we are called upon to resolve. Though sometimes difficult, dynamic aspects can be productive of genuine personal growth, if we rise to the challenges they represent.

Conjunction

The *conjunction* (♂) of two planets produces a blending of the planetary energies involved and usually they operate as a powerful combined force. A person with several conjunctions in the birthchart is likely to be highly focused and have personal power. Conjunctions can be regarded as either flowing or dynamic depending on the nature of the planets involved.

Sextile

The *sextile* (⚹) indicates a harmonious association of the two planets. A birthchart with sextile aspects predominating is indicative of an easygoing, free-and-easy nature that avoids challenges wherever possible.

Square

The *square* (□) produces conflict that demands some form of effort at reconciliation or productive growth. Too many squares and you have someone who thrives on difficulty!

TRINE

The *trine* (△) is a strongly harmonious aspect that often denotes some form of natural talent or good fortune in the areas concerned. An abundance of trines in a birthchart may indicate laziness or taking good fortune for granted.

OPPOSITION

The *opposition* (☍) often produces a see-saw effect, with one planet gaining dominance at the expense of the other, until awareness and understanding of one's own psychological patterns enables one to accept one's own internal contradictions. Often with an opposition aspect, we tend to identify with one planet and project the qualities of the opposing planet on to someone else. Many oppositions in a birthchart may indicate disruptive relationships.

ASPECT PATTERNS

These are configurations of multiple aspects that have a particular meaning in themselves. For instance, three or more planets in conjunction form a *Stellium* (Figure 8), which indicates a powerful focus of energies in the sign and House in which it is located.

Figure 8 Example Stellium

A *Grand Trine* occurs when three planets trine each other, forming an equilateral triangle (Figure 9). A Grand Trine indicates an easy flow of energies between all three planets that often corresponds to

a particular set of talents according to which planets are involved, though such talents may in some senses be too easy and taken for granted. For instance, a grand trine between Sun, Mars and Jupiter indicates great energy and enthusiasm, though it may not be directed constructively or may lead to activity for its own sake.

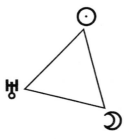

Figure 9 Example Grand Trine

An opposition aspect, where a third planet is midway between the two opposing planets (and square to both) is called a *T-square* (Figure 10). This can produce much conflict and exaggerate the functioning of the midway (or *focal*) planet. The energies symbolised by the focal planet need to be used wisely and consciously in order to avoid compulsive or excessive activity.

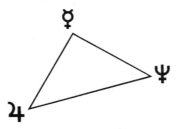

Figure 10 Example T-square

A *Grand Cross* occurs when two opposition aspects are at right angles to each other and all four planets (or more, if conjunctions are also involved) are square to each other (Figure 11). This aspect pattern indicates the tendency to be pulled in many directions at

once, creating internal tension or division. However, people with this pattern in their birthcharts can be highly effective when they stop fighting themselves and the outside world and instead concentrate their energies internally. They are then capable of acting with great purpose from a calm centre rather than being tossed around on a sea of conflicting desires.

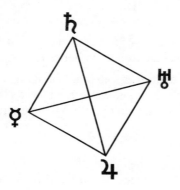

Figure 11 Example Grand Cross

Chart Themes

In many birthcharts, there are often repeated patterns or *chart themes*. These can reflect important issues that are especially important in the life of the individual. For instance, a planet may be in a sign and also in aspect to the ruler of that sign, in which case you have a 'double whammy', to borrow a phrase from Stephen Arroyo, in his delightful and informative guide to synastry, *Relationships and Life Cycles* (see Appendix 2). If the second planet is also in a sign ruled by the first, you have a 'triple whammy'. An example would be Mars in Taurus opposite Venus in Scorpio, in which case you have a triple 'Mars/Venus' theme, with the consequence that sexual relationships (and perhaps complications caused by them) are an important theme in the person's life. Sometimes you find that a horoscope contains several such themes.

Aspect keywords

Following are interpretations of each of the aspects.

Conjunctions (☌) are listed separately, though for reasons of space, the sextiles (⚹) and trines (△) are listed together, as are the squares (□) and oppositions (☍). The squares and oppositions are divided into negative (–) and positive (+) manifestations.

For a fuller understanding of the aspects, you are recommended to read *Planets in Aspect* by Robert Pelletier (see Appendix 2).

Remember that these are possible manifestations only, intended to stimulate you to discover other ways in which the two planetary principles could manifest, using your own experience of life as a guide.

PRACTICE

Where you find dynamic aspects in your own chart, ask yourself whether this part of you has caused problems in the past. If so, did you resolve them, and how? Did they bring about any constructive changes? Did they provoke you to do things differently? What did you learn?

SUN ASPECTS

☉ / ☽ ☌: Confident; lively; creative; whole; subjective; self-involved; spontaneous; joyful. ⚹/△: Balanced; happy; adaptable; parental harmony; sincere; equilibrium. □/☍: – Inner tension; conflict between conscious mind and emotions; parental disharmony. + Gifted; self-knowledge; strength of character; creativity.

☉ / ASC ☌: Confident; outgoing; extrovert; energetic; lively; cheerful; attention-seeking; winning; open; direct; positive. ⚹/△: Popular; confidence; positive; recognised; public; optimistic; sunny disposition. □/☍: – Egotistical; pushy; over-confident; misunderstood; uncompromising. + Direct; honest; strong personality; character; conscious self-expression.

☉ / ☿ ♂: Intelligent; witty; well-read; talkative; self-centred; curious; confident communicator; humorous. ✳/△: *No aspect possible in birthchart.* □/☍: *No aspect possible in birthchart.*

☉ / ♀: Popular; attractive; beautiful; active social life; romantic; artistic; stylish, taste; harmonious; indulgent; refined; affectionate. ✳/△: *No aspect possible in birthchart.* □/☍: *No aspect possible in birthchart.*

☉ / ♂ ♂: Strong ego; forceful; energetic; impulsive; competitive; leadership; decisive; courageous; anger; sexual energy; ego-battles. ✳/△: Vitality; confidence; determination; active; enterprising; healthy aggression; decisive; constructive. □/☍: – Combative; headstrong; pushy; over-active; restless; hot temper; disputes; difficult men. + Ambitious; daring; brave; competitive; sexual energy; dynamic; sport; successful activity.

☉ / MC ♂: Ambition; confidence; fame; purpose; public attention; authority; success; creative career; self-importance. ✳/△: Consciousness of aim in life; successful; aspiring; self-knowledge; positive; ambitious; individual. □/☍: – Arrogant; egocentric; conflict with authorities; pulled between home and career. + Ambitious; sacrifices for career/goals; fame; recognition; honours; vocation.

☉ / ♃ ♂: Fortunate; successful; philosophical; generous; positive; conceited; learning; liberal; travel; undisciplined; teaching. ✳/△: Happy; confident; popular; genial; easy-going; good health; promotion; lucky; travel; altruistic; learning; opportunities. □/☍: – Spendthrift; arrogant; ostentatious; over-zealous; excess; religious or legal conflicts. + Wealth; wisdom; success; positivity; many opportunities.

☉ / ♄ ♂: Self-disciplined; responsible; serious; strong father; hard-working; need to prove oneself; self-doubting; realistic. ✳/△: Responsible; determined; trusted; consistent; conservative; reserved; hard work; gradual advancement. □/☍: – Inhibited; difficulties with father; inferiority complex; fearful; workaholic; rigid; self-critical; health problems. + Accomplished; self-disciplined; high standards; business skills; achievement.

☉ / ♅ ♂: Individualistic; headstrong; independent; unconventional; rebellious; progressive; inventive; radical; original; genius; erratic. ⚹/△: Individual; independent; magnetic; love of change; creative; open-minded; intuitive; reforming. □/♂⃝: – Rebellious; wild; shocking; alienated; eccentric; anarchic; disruptive; accident-prone; nervous; unstable. + Reforming; intuitive; politics; embraces change; challenges status quo.

☉ / ♆ ♂: Imaginative; impressionable; compassionate; visionary; weak ego; artistic; inspired; idealistic musical; escapist; mysticism; intuitive; martyrdom. ⚹/△: Open; idealistic; relaxed attitude to life; understanding; kind; creative; imaginative; art; music; poetry. □/♂⃝: – Escapist; confused; victim-consciousness; fantasies; illusions; self-loss. + Vivid inner life; psychic or mystical experiences; visionary; artistic; spiritual growth.

☉ / ♇ ♂: Powerful ego; great ambition; dominating; transformations; ruthless; hunter/hunted; hypnotic; obsessive; self-destruction; creative power. ⚹/△: Influential; leading; creative power; major changes; recuperative strength; striving for power. □/♂⃝: – Autocratic; fate; power struggles; self-destruction; explosive; survival tests; cruel or absent father. + Transformations; empowerment; mastery; personal power.

☉ / ☊ ♂: Growth through creativity and leadership; popularity; creative associations; talent; ability to perform at a high level; personal growth; self-discovery. ⚹/△: Personal growth; leadership potential; creative and intellectual contacts; motivation; self-development. □/♂⃝: – Conflict between fulfilment and ego needs; creative block; short-lived relationships. + Leadership; creativity; ability to perform at a high level.

MOON ASPECTS

☽ / ASC ♂: Warm personality; caring; sensitive; emotional; moody; changeable; sympathetic; living near water; needs security; habitual. ⚹/△: Warm; obliging; adaptable; sympathetic; hospitable; good relations with women; supportive; need to belong; caring; parental. □/♂⃝: – Oversensitive; touchy; withdrawal; outbursts; insecure;

sentimental; smothering. + Warm; strong feelings; caring for others; parenting; strong family life.

☽ / ☿ ♂: Communicating feelings; understanding; changeable; reflective; irrational; talkative; imaginative; non-verbal communication. ⚹/△: Articulate; good judgement; adaptable; sympathetic; perceptive; communication with women; approachable. □/☍: – Voluble; gossip; nervous; irrational; sensitive to criticism; misunderstandings; trivia; insecure. + Wit; insightful; able to verbalise feelings; sensitive communicator; eloquence.

☽ / ♀ ♂: Affectionate; pleasure-loving; romantic; self-indulgent; artistic; beautiful home; hospitable; loving; female friends; cultured; happy marriage; comfortable; fawning. ⚹/△: Relaxed; tasteful; easy-going; artistic; refined; hospitable; attractive home; well-liked. □/☍: – Over-indulgent; bad taste; cloying; sentimental; needy; fear of rejection. + Loving; close friendships; grace; beautifying environment; caring lover.

☽ / ♂ ♂: Impulsive; tense; hot temper; volatile; irritable; inner strength; strong feelings; defensive; family discord; strong mother. ⚹/△: Inner strength; guts; sincere; protective; actively caring; involved; assertive; busy; strong women; teamwork. □/☍: – Irritable; easily upset; volatile; bad-tempered; difficulties with women; defensive; domestic turbulence. + Strong will; protective; bravery; actively caring.

☽ / MC ♂: Caring profession; women in the public eye; rewarding career; changing goals; caring public image; career/family links. ⚹/△: Caring attitude to work; family values; love of home; sensitive to public; land; roots; career and home balanced. □/☍: – Fluctuating goals; avoiding the limelight; attachment to past; conflict between home and work. + Caring or emotionally rewarding work; vocation; in touch with public mood.

☽ / ♃ ♂: Generous; fortunate; faith; cheerful; home abroad; luxurious home; gluttony; waste; good upbringing; tolerant; travel; wealthy women; good relationship to women. ⚹/△: Emotional richness; tolerant; happy mother; good-humoured; positive; large family; altruistic; sincere; happy marriage. □/☍: – Extravagant;

excess; over-eating and drinking; excess of emotion. + Generous; exuberant; benevolent; caring for many; good fortune.

☽ / ♄ ♂: Emotional maturity; self-controlled; dutiful; family responsibilities; strict mother; hard-working; professional; self-critical. ✶/△: Realism; wisdom; wise mother; responsible; harmony between home and work; emotional maturity. □/⚼: – Inhibitions; difficulties with mother; depression; family burdens; controlling; home *vs.* career. + Emotional depth; inner strength; mastery of emotions; dedication.

☽ / ♅ ♂: Independent; unconventional family life; magnetic; highly strung; eccentric; wilful; restless; bohemian; unconventional women. ✶/△: Intuitive; unusual family/home life; spontaneous; lively; alert; modern home; emotionally independent; creative. □/⚼: – Extreme independence; volatile; highly strung; mood swings; excitable; unstable home life; upsets; radical women; eccentric. + Liberated; exciting lifestyle; free; highly creative.

☽ / ♆ ♂: Sensitive; imaginative; dreamy; romantic; gentle; spiritual; artistic; vague; lazy; intuitive; deceptive; sensitive mother. ✶/△: Compassionate; open; imaginative; gentle; understanding; empathetic; relaxed; receptive; art. □/⚼: – Hypersensitive; weak; confused; addictive; self-deception; mediumistic; martyrdom; escapist; delusions. + Spiritualised emotions; compassion; healing; spiritual experience.

☽ / ♀ ♂: Emotionally intense; powerful mother; deep feelings; moody; hidden feelings; self-destructive; demanding; survival; craving for intimacy. ✶/△: Intense emotions; deep; intense; tough love; instinct; intimacy; powerful women. □/⚼: – Emotional upheavals; obsessive relationships; tormented; jealous; demanding; manipulation. + Emotional depth; emotional honesty; purging the past; survival.

☽ / ☊ ♂: Growth through development of feelings or parenthood; caring for others; emotional fulfilment; women encourage growth; inner richness; depth. ✶/△: Nurturing one's potential; inner relationships; supportive family; associations of women. □/⚼: – Lack of adaptability; difficulties with family; habit or comfort impedes growth; negativity; griping; attachment to past. + Exploration of emotions; self-discovery; inner fulfilment.

ASCENDANT ASPECTS

ASC / ☿ ♂: Intelligent personality; humorous; quick-witted; communicative; voluble; articulate; lively; mobile; intellectual; writing; sociable; travel; fluent; adaptable. ✳/△: Sociable; communicative; many contacts; articulate; friendly; verbal; fluent; writing, mobile. □/☍: – Gossip; superficial; frivolous; anxious; misunderstandings; talkative; edgy; practical jokes; insincere. + Intellectual; stimulating; polished; skilled communicator; wit.

ASC / ♀ ♂: Attractive personality; beauty; charm; sexy; vain; popular; sociable; friendly; fashionable; stylish; art; music; harmonious. ✳/△: Graceful; attractive personality; harmonious; relaxed; easy-going; good taste; cultured; diplomatic. □/☍: – Disharmonious attitude; vain; self-indulgent; difficulties in relationships; playing on one's charm; shallow; flighty; bad taste; ostentatious. + Style; polish; artistry; loving marriage; attractive partner.

ASC / ♂ ♂: Forceful personality; tough; assertive; blunt; leading; decisive; courageous; energetic; physical strength; competitive; athletic; sport. ✳/△: Energy; strength; courage; self-assertion; forceful; frank; robust; active life; team-work; sports; athletic; healthy; vital. □/☍: – Aggressive personality; rough; crude; fighting; disagreements; rash; marital tensions. + Courage; physical strength; daring; dynamic relationships; strong partner.

ASC / MC ♂: *No aspect possible in birthchart.* ✳/△: Integration, harmony between public and private selves; smooth passage through life. □ only: – Conflict between public and private selves; gap between actuality and aims; lack of direction; difficult passage through life. + Conscious integration of self; striving for integrity.

ASC / ♃ ♂: Expansive personality; confident; positive; jovial; renowned; weight-gain; widely travelled; successful; self-important; benevolent; educated; principled. ✳/△: Positive; respected; fun; good reputation; cheerful; co-operative; happy marriage; good company. □/☍: – Arrogant; extravagance; bragging; pompous; self-indulgent; multiple relationships. + Exuberant; travel; adventure; wealthy partner; fortunate marriage.

ASC / ♄ ♂: Serious personality; professional front; inhibited; lonely; unconfident; self-critical; duty; productive; sensible; anxious; austere. ✳/△: Mature; responsible; serious; experienced; hard-working; cautious; sensible; respected; stable marriage; economical; integrity; established. □/♂: – Inhibited personality; separations; self-critical; workaholic; excessive discipline. + Achievement; professional; older partner; long-lasting marriage.

ASC / ♅ ♂: Exciting personality; dynamic; radical; headstrong; unconventional; inventive; challenging; progressive; unusual appearance; bohemian; rebellious. ✳/△: Individual; quick; changeable; wacky; creative; modern; independent; adventurous. □/♂: – Upsets; shocking; alienated; accidents; eccentric; short-lived relationships; wild; disruptive; thrill-seeking. + Catalyst; free spirit; inventive; brilliant; unusual partner.

ASC / ♆ ♂: Sensitive personality; imaginative; open; charismatic; magical; gentle; shy; romantic image; intuitive; escapist; artistic; spiritual; selfless; acting. ✳/△: Understanding; refined; sympathetic; flowing; relaxed; artistic; intuitive relationships. □/♂: – Hypersensitive; confused; vulnerable; escapist; amorphous; self-denying; martyrdom. + Sympathetic; imaginative; spiritual; sensitive or artistic partner.

ASC / ♇ ♂: Powerful personality; fascinating; dominating; hypnotic; dictatorial; dramatic; influential; great changes; willpower. ✳/△: Strong personality; personal power; stamina; leading; transformative; effective; deep relationships; rebuilding. □/♂: – Anti-social; disruptive; violent; insatiable; dangerous environments; obsessive. + Transformations; powerful partner; charisma; survival.

ASC / ☊ ♂: Growth through development of personality; sociable; many friends; fellowship. ✳/△: Easy growth; manifestation of potential; shared interests; fulfilment; development of the personality; growth through relationships. □/♂: – Difficult growth; discordant self-projection; growth *vs.* relationships; struggle for fulfilment; dissatisfied. + Growth through marriage or partnership; overcoming challenges to growth.

MERCURY ASPECTS

☿ / ♀ ♂: Sociable; charming; eloquent; agreeable; social graces; poetic; writing skills; musical; witty; cultured; facile; fair-minded; easy-going; pleasant; tactful. ✶ only: Sociable; cultured; light-hearted; hilarity; literary skill; leisured; witty; decorous; diplomatic; liked; friendly; co-operative; polished. □/♂°: *No aspect possible in birthchart.*

☿ / ♂ ♂: Mentally assertive; resourceful; outspoken; forceful speaker; enterprising; argumentative; decisive; impatient; sharp intellect; nervous energy. ✶/△: Decisive; quick; sceptical; repartee; enterprise; debate; mentally active; good negotiator; frank. □/♂°: − Argumentative; sarcastic; cutting; rash; hurtful; nervous energy; hot-headed; headaches. + Mental strength; debating skills; sharp mind; intellectual daring; pioneering ideas.

☿ / MC ♂: Intellectual career; communications; eloquent; the media; well travelled; well-informed; flexible aims; writing, teaching. ✶/△: Planned career; self-knowledge; thinking ahead; flexible in work; good career contacts; networking. □/♂°: − Many jobs or careers; changes of direction; difficulty communicating with family or employers; public or professional gossip. + Publishing; authorship; the media; lively home life.

☿ / ♃ ♂: Positive mentality; humorous; well-educated; literary; well-travelled; fluent; honest; broadcasting; many interests; sloppy; philosophy; teaching. ✶/△: Broad-minded; constructive; knowledgeable; writing; confident speaker; travel; busy; good humoured. □/♂°: − Loud; verbose; arrogant; excessive travel; philosophical or religious disputes. + Encyclopaedic knowledge; gifted orator; successful writing; many fortunate contacts.

☿ / ♄ ♂: Serious-minded; pessimistic; studious; pragmatic; slow; logical; painstaking; organised; conformist; eye for detail; planning; business skills. ✶/△: Organised; methodical; efficient; researching; thorough; planning skills; common sense; good judgement. □/♂°: − Negative thinking; narrow; anxious; speech difficulties; slow learner; overly logical; laboured. + Executive ability; intellectual authority; mastery of detail.

☿ / ♅ ♂: Original mind; brilliant; inventive; quick; unusual ideas; science; maths; information technology; misunderstood; rapid speech. ✳/△: Quick mind; inventive; wit; progressive; information technology; stimulating; puzzles; sudden journeys. □/♂°: – Hasty or nervous speech; nervous strain; arrogant; inability to relax; impulsive; crazy ideas; upsets; accidents. + Genius; scientific insights; challenging; inventions.

☿ / ♆ ♂: Imaginative; creative mind; inspired; intuitive; vague; the unconscious mind; fiction; dreamy; spiritual knowledge; poetic; visionary. ✳/△: Imaginative; understanding; poetic; fantasy; visualisation; hunches; images. □/♂°: – Confused; over-imaginative; absent-minded; deception; delusions; anxiety; untruths; hallucinations. + Highly intuitive; poetic and literary skills; visionary; psychic; magical stories; aura reading.

☿ / ♀ ♂: Penetrating intellect; persuasive; mentally dominating; secretive; fascinating; love of mysteries; psychology; highly analytical; cynical; nobody's fool. ✳/△: Intellectual power; convincing; observant; researching; study; psychology; insightful. □/♂°: – Propaganda; obsessive; sarcastic; acid; secretive; cunning; intellectual power struggles. + Powerful intellect; highly influential ideas; profound insight; uncovering truth.

☿ / ☊ ♂: Growth through development of intellect; authorship; communication skills; creative mind; new ideas; sharing ideas; intellectual associations. ✳/△: Intellectual interests; growth through communication; sociable; joint interests; fellowship. □/♂°: – Sceptical; superficial activities; intellectualising; intellectualism *vs.* growth; thinking about potential *vs.* manifesting it. + Intellectual development; oratory; communication gifts.

VENUS ASPECTS

♀ / ♂ ♂: Passionate; highly sexed; animal magnetism; sexy; coarse; prolific; desire; love/hate relationships; lively; *joie de vivre*; stormy relationships; dynamic art. ✳/△: Healthy sex drive; fun-loving; sensual; creative; desire; procreation; warm; creative energies. □/♂°: – Stormy relationships; sexually competitive; unfaithful; bad taste; over-sexed; love *vs.* sex; exploitation. + Highly creative; fulfilling sex life; youthful.

♀ / MC ♂: Artistic career; good public relations; professional women; creativity; loved by many; beauty industry; the arts; social skills; social ambition. ✳/△: Enjoys work; popular; good contacts; parents as friends; good relationship to authority; teamwork. □/♂°: – Desire to succeed without effort; seeks celebrity; vain; dependent on others; pleasure *vs.* work. + Artistic success; adored by public; trendsetter; style guru.

♀ / ♃ ♂: Many friends and lovers; extravagant; hedonistic; ostentatious; larger than life; celebrity; luxury; religious art; foreign or wealthy friends; love of learning. ✳/△: Many friends; charming; gain through friends; happiness in love; good times; creative; over-eating; generous. □/♂°: – Unfaithful; extravagant; vain; ostentatious; over-indulgence; weight gain; excess; pretence. + Abundance; joy; loved by many; philanthropy; successful art.

♀ / ♄ ♂: Loyal; restrained affections; lonely; older friends and lovers; practical; seeks security; enjoys work; social status; formal or conventional art. ✳/△: Sober; dutiful; fidelity; mature in love; experienced; good relationships at work. □/♂°: – Separations; fear of rejection; lack of self-worth; creative struggle; guilt trips; money troubles. + Long-lasting marriage; formal art skills (architecture; sculpture, drawing, design), earned self-worth.

♀ / ♅ ♂: Magnetic; exciting; popular; free love; short-lived relationships; unconventional tastes; avant-garde; sparkling personality; bohemian. ✳/△: Exciting relationships; original art; rhythm; style; unpossessive; creative; uninhibited; cool. □/♂°: – Unstable relationships; love of shocking; eccentric friends and lovers; capricious; fear of intimacy. + Sexual liberation; creative genius; style guru; musical skills.

♀ / ♆ ♂: Spiritual love; artistic; musical; refined; imaginative; visionary art; trusting; compassionate; attracted to imaginative, religious or helpless types. ✳/△: Refined; artistic; musical; erotic imagination; idealised love; creative; diffuse affections; lazy. □/♂°: – Romantic illusions; pornography; secret love; unrealistic expectations; scandal; avoiding relationship. + Spiritual love; artistic inspiration; beautiful soul; compassion.

♀ / ♀ ♂: Passionate; intense attractions; sexual magnetism; lustful; possessive; influential; intense creativity; powerful friends and

lovers. ✶/△: Passionate relationships; creative power; magnetic; procreation; fated meetings; strong values. □/♂°: – Fanatical love affairs; lust; domination and submission; destructive friends and lovers; insatiable; possessive. + Deeply enriching relationships; soul unions; passionate creativity; prolific.

♀ / ☊ ♂: Growth through relationships, love or creativity; happy marriage; attractive personality; wealth creation; artistic associations; groups of women; fortunate friendships; charm. ✶/△: Fulfilment through love; creative relationships; enjoyment of personal growth. □/♂°: – Social life conflicts with growth potential; laziness encourages stagnation; relationships as escape from inner conflict. + Fulfilment though love; artistically gifted.

MARS ASPECTS

♂ / ♃ ♂: Highly active; sporting; confident; entrepreneurial; honourable; fit; athletic; adventurous; arrogant; philosophical conflicts; sexual energy. ✶/△: Energetic; frank; spirited; sporting; healthy ambition; strength; bonhomie; ambitious; travel. □/♂°: – Arrogance; over-confidence; zealous; rebellious; manic; rude; reckless; problems abroad; gambling. + Sporting success; success through positivity; risk-taking; heroism.

♂ / ♄ ♂: Hard-working; endurance; hard; effort; self-disciplined; fear of weakness; frustrated; engineering; economical; strong-willed. ✶/△: Constructive activity; tough; disciplined; hard-working; determined; focused; practical skills; stamina. □/♂°: – Frustrated; restriction; suppressed anger; difficulties with father; bullying; negative re-enforcement. + Great achievements through effort; physical endurance; focused energy.

♂ / ♅ ♂: Rebellious; seeks freedom; wilful; accidents; assertive; impulsive; dynamic; adventurous; speed; daring; foolhardy. ✶/△: Independent; decisive; leading; mechanical skills (vehicles, engines, etc.); adventurous; exciting; enterprising; sexual energy. □/♂°: – Trouble-making; reckless; accident prone; seeks danger; revolutionary; tantrums; explosions. + Fights oppression; asserts freedom; catalyst; racing.

♂ / ♆ ♂: Spiritually or artistically active; romantic; sexual fantasies; lethargic; escapist; imaginative; active compassion; causes; sense of

rhythm. ✶/△: Creative activity; courage of ideals; inspired actions; dance; martial arts; rhythm. □/☍: – Dissolute; escapist; impotent; defeatist; low vitality; weak; apathetic; sexual addiction. + Heroism; spiritual leadership; transcendence of desire; personal magnetism.

♂ / ♀ ♂: Power; great ambition; aggression; brutal; excessive effort; dominance; survival; destruction; explosive; obsessive. ✶/△: Sexual energy; great efforts; courageous; untiring; ambitious; regeneration; intense; athletic; will power; survival instinct. □/☍: – Extremist; explosive; lust for power; ruthless; violent; obsessive; voracious; bullying. + Superhuman force; fighting oppression; great courage.

♂ / ♌ ♂: Growth through activity/self-assertion/sex; concentration on goals; courageous; enterprising; sport; athletics; wholesome; camaraderie; collaboration; team spirit. ✶/△: Assertiveness aids growth; energetic associations; comradeship; team spirit; vigour; whole-hearted; shared pursuits and successes. □/☍: – Tension caused by desire to grow; obstacles; challenges; irritability; conflicts caused by personal growth. + Overcoming challenges to growth; rising to challenges; talents displayed in adversity.

MIDHEAVEN ASPECTS

MC / ♃ ♂: Successful; fortunate; many opportunities; vocation; public confidence; prominence; religious; ethical; well-travelled; success abroad; recognised. ✶/△: Career fulfilment; motivated; humane; confident; happy family life; good relationship to authority; enterprising; large home. □/☍: – Over-estimation of abilities; over-ambitious; ostentatious; pompous; preaching; inflated ego. + Great success; fame; great faith.

MC / ♄ ♂: Slow but sure advancement; ambitious; hard-working; late starter; determined; respected; integrity; public duty; authoritative; professional. ✶/△: Commitment to goals; experienced; hard-working; trusted; clear goals. □/☍: – Fear of failure; obstacles; torn between work and home; workaholic; fear of public exposure; family responsibilities. + Executive ability; wise; overcoming obstacles; great integrity.

MC / ♅ ♂: Unusual career; exciting life; extraordinary aims; visionary; sudden success; radical; catalyst; technological or scientific career; infamy; futuristic. ✶/△: Unusual aims or working methods; dynamic; science/technology; sudden opportunities. □/☍: – Chequered career; unsettled home life; rebellious; radical public image; rebellion against expectations. + Meteoric rise; fighting oppression; inventions; scientific progress.

MC / ♆ ♂: Imaginative, artistic or caring career; unambitious; aimless; utopian; vocation; glamorous; service to humanity; public compassion; films. ✶/△: Compassion or imagination in career; films/art/music; fashion; easy-going attitude to work; idealistic; lazy about goals. □/☍: – Lack of direction; confused goals; fear of exposure; self-doubt. + Spiritual or humanitarian work; dedication; artistic achievement; charitable work.

MC / ♀ ♂: Great ambition; fame; demanding career; twists of fate; authority; great changes of fortune; notoriety; dislike of officialdom; vocation. ✶/△: Authoritative; influential; enterprising; determination; expert knowledge; moral authority. □/☍: – Extreme ambition; disrupted childhood; conflict with authorities; autocratic.
+ Extraordinary achievements; changing the world; revolutionary; destiny.

MC / ☊ ♂: Growth through career or public visibility; public contacts; fame; providence; desire for security; emotional attachments; clinging. ✶/△: Talented; exploiting one's gifts in career; advancement; sharing one's gifts with the world. □/☍: – Self-interest *vs.* collective interest; conflict between career and true path in life. + Public success; fame; a gift to the world.

JUPITER ASPECTS

♃ / ♄ ♂: Long-term goals; patient; love of hard work; deserved success; manic depressive; ponderous; responsible; ethical; purposeful; respected. ✶/△: Earned success; honourable; patient; industrious; integrity; business ability; right action. □/☍: – Restless; tested; irresponsible; moral conflicts; missed opportunities; work *vs.* fun; rigid ideals. + Search for meaning; deeply questioning; great integrity; wise.

♃ / ♅ ♂: Freedom-loving; eclectic; unorthodox ideas or beliefs; visionary; futuristic; adventurous; challenging; causes; speculation; inventive; lucky breaks. ✳/△: Original; ingenious; freedom-loving; progressive; liberal; flair; questioning. □/♂°: – Religious or philosophical conflicts; anarchy; inability to slow down; wild; gambling; eccentric beliefs; reckless. + Challenges convention; liberated; brilliant inventions; successful campaigning.

♃ / ♆ ♂: Visionary; humanitarian; compassionate; imaginative; spiritual growth; selfless; tolerant; religious; gambling; impractical; creativity; metaphysics; cults. ✳/△: Idealistic; humane; kind; philanthropic; faith; gain without effort; flowing; tolerant. □/♂°: – Drifting; gambling; waste; zealous religiosity; irresponsible; addictive; excessive spirituality. + Spiritual experiences; foreknowledge; philanthropy; bliss.

♃ / ♀ ♂: Financial success; accomplishments; big ideas; regeneration; desire for fame; discovery of faith; free enterprise; self-betterment; campaigning. ✳/△: Leading; social regeneration; financial successes; organising skills; resourceful; convincing; control over one's life. □/♂°: – Gambling; power struggles; grandiose claims; fanatical. + Successful enterprises; great reforms; wealth creation; religious conversion.

♃ / ☊ ♂: Growth through confidence; broadening one's horizons through travel or higher education; adventures; exploration of potential. ✳/△: Confident about potential; good connections; educational interests; personal growth; fulfilment; joy; gain through talent. □/♂°: – Personal growth as a religion; fun *vs.* developing one's own potential; waste of talent. + Multi-talented, self-realisation; faith in one's individual path in life.

SATURN ASPECTS

♄ / ♅ ♂: Constructive; practical reforms; struggle for freedom; political thought; technical skills; internal tensions; suppressed individuality. ✳/△: Organised; systematic; capable; tough-minded; unusual working methods; structured change or reform. □/♂°: – Limitation of freedom; physical tension; conflict with authority; conformist;

reactionary. + Scientific breakthroughs; political insight; reform of outdated methods or structures.

♄ / ♆ ♂: Practical spirituality; ascetic; sensitive to suffering; spiritual maturity; wisdom; prayer; healing; retreat; sadness; crisis of faith; paranoia. ⚹/△: Self-sacrifice; patient; behind-the-scenes work; meditation; helping; healing; practical idealism; reflective; monastic. □/♂: – Anxious; neurotic; over-sensitive; depressive; negative; suffering; lethargic; illness. + Charity; healing; self-sacrifice; wisdom; ethical living.

♄ / ♀ ♂: Tough; indestructible; struggle; deep transformations; secretive; researching; brutal; determined; authoritative; obsessive. ⚹/△: Difficult work; great achievements; tough; self-discipline; work done in isolation or in secret; resourceful; economical. □/♂: – Hardship; cruelty; self-destructive; dictatorial; extreme ambition; compulsion. + Overcoming great obstacles; feats of endurance; self-mastery; deep transformations.

♄ / ☊ ♂: Growth through work; struggle to manifest potential; depth; success with effort; the necessity to be true to oneself. ⚹/△: Work aids personal growth; sponsorship from elderly or established people; mature; deep fulfilment. □/♂: – Struggle to achieve potential; pessimism; separations; inhibited social function; attachment to suffering; isolated. + Self-knowledge; vocation; fulfilment of goals; understanding the past.

URANUS ASPECTS

♅ / ♆ ♂: Spiritual freedom; enlightenment; virtual reality; unusual states of mind; global awareness; flux; paradigm shifts; global politics; crazy wisdom. ⚹/△: Vivid dreams; flashes of enlightenment; spiritual groups; surreal; magical. □/♂: – Impossible ideals; psychic confusion; weird states of mind; the paranormal; hallucinations; alienated. + Insight into the unconscious; illumination; amazing discoveries; precognition.

♅ / ♀ ♂: Revolutionary; radical; overthrow of the old order; cultural revolution; intense creativity; chaos; anti-authoritarian; mass movements; mutation. ⚹/△: Reforming; progressive; creation of the new; pioneering; restless; pushing back frontiers. □/♂: –

Revolutionary; destruction; chaos; mobs; subversion; limitation of freedom; destructive science. + Resisting oppression; reforms to society; birth of a new order; creative change.

♅ / ☊ ☌: Growth through experimentation; unusual talents; development of individuality; innovative; study of patterns, rhythms and cycles. ⚹/△: Innovation aids growth; technological development; seeks variety; humanitarian pursuits. □/☍: – Dilettante; desire for freedom vs. growth; thrill-seeking; unthinking radicalism; difficulty finishing anything. + Brilliance; sudden development; highly unusual gifts; growth spurts.

NEPTUNE ASPECTS

♆ / ☿ ☌: Spiritual transformation; mass movements; powerful imagination; collective myths; death wish; hypnotism; magical power. ⚹/△: Inner life; active imagination; spiritual growth; mysticism; the supernatural; self-knowledge. □/☍: – Madness unleashed; abuse of psychic power; zealotry; fundamentalism; collective hallucinations. + Spiritual regeneration; psychological death and rebirth.

♆ / ☊ ☌: Growth through spirituality; development of imagination; spiritual groups; wisdom; joy; art and music; compassion; inner riches. ⚹/△: Imagination aids growth; humanitarian and utopian organisations; love of magic and mysticism; development of artistic abilities. □/☍: – Apathy; waste of potential fear of development; dreaming replacing growth. + Spiritual or artistic gifts; divine guidance; spiritual wisdom.

PLUTO ASPECTS

♇ / ☊ ☌: Growth through power; psychological development; powerful friends or associations; destined; understanding of current trends; contact with the masses. ⚹/△: Regeneration aids growth; ambition; growth through exercise of power; reform. □/☍: – Power vs. growth; self-obsession; held back; fear of development; frustration. + Seizing the moment; huge strides to growth; wielding great influence with others.

horoscope
interpretation

N ow you are familiar with the individual elements of a horoscope, you can begin to interpret a complete birthchart. You will find yourself getting a feel for the individual's personality and the challenges he or she faces. In short, you start to discover the person in the horoscope.

Remember that all the keywords in Chapter 3 are only pointers to what, in reality, are living 'energies' that exist within each of us. These energies are what make up a human personality, not a series of easily understood, clear-cut labels. Like any label or description, they are not the thing itself. It is one of the joys of astrology that, once familiar with its language, you begin to experience the astrological dynamics that are just beneath the surface of everyday encounters or situations. You can see more clearly where people's behaviour and actions are 'coming from'.

Interpretation guidelines

A horoscope often reveals such a mass of information that it is a good idea to have a framework for interpreting it. Aim to find the most important elements of the birthchart first. Once you have those, you can then explore the details.

The best place to start is by looking at the sign positions of the:

1 Sun
2 Moon
3 Ascendant

These three points form the basis of the personality; much insight can be gained from these alone.

Next, take in a general picture of the horoscope by noting the following factors:

4   Distribution of planets by *polarity*: how many planets in negative signs, how many in positive?
5   Distribution by Element (triplicity): How many planets in Fire, Air, Water or Earth signs?
6   Distribution by mode (quadruplicity): How many planets in Cardinal (Aries, Cancer, Libra, Capricorn), Fixed (Taurus, Leo, Scorpio, Aquarius) or Mutable (Gemini, Virgo, Sagittarius, Pisces) signs?
7   Distribution by House mode: How many planets in Angular (I, IV, VII, X), Succedent (II, V, VIII, XI) or Cadent (III, VI, IX, XII) houses?
8   Planets in rulership or detriment
9   Major aspect patterns (Stellium, T-square, Grand Trine, Grand Cross)
10 Most tenanted Houses
11 Most tenanted signs
12 Chart themes
13 Ruler of the Ascendant

The above will give you a general view of the horoscope. Now you can look at the nature of each planet in more detail, taking account of its sign, aspects and House positions.

14 Sun, Moon and Ascendant: The basis of the personality
15 Mercury, Venus and Mars: Communication and relationships
16 Midheaven, Jupiter and Saturn: Relationship to society
17 The Moon's North Node: The path to fulfilment
18 Uranus, Neptune and Pluto: Generational influences

Remember that the outer planets will be more influential if strongly aspected by the Sun, Moon, Asc, personal planets or the MC.

Now you have of a clearer picture of the person, stay with the feelings and images the horoscope evokes. Get a feel for what kind of person this is, and how he or she may behave. Visualise what the person looks like, how he or she speaks and moves, the kind of words used, what feelings the person has in different situations.

Different 'takes'

When you have drawn up several birthcharts for people you know, you can then focus on different 'takes' on their birthcharts, like a director shooting a scene from different angles. For instance, you could look at the birthchart in terms of career potential, by focusing on the Sun, Midheaven (and aspects to them) and the IInd, VIth and Xth Houses and their rulers.

Alternatively, you might look at the birthchart in terms of relationships. What does this person look for in a relationship, what type is he or she attracted to? What problems are likely to crop up? This could involve exploring the Moon, Venus and Mars (and aspects to them) as well as the Vth and VIIth Houses and their rulers.

Every horoscope tells a different story and has many layers of meaning. Interpretation is the art of teasing out this story, often through letting its symbols playfully work on us.

PRACTICE

Interpret Jimi Hendrix's birthchart in Chapter 2.

Astrological consultation

People have a consultation with an astrologer for a variety of reasons. Some do it out of curiosity, simply wanting to know a little more about themselves or astrology.

Many people seeking an astrologer's advice are at a crossroads in their lives and are seeking guidance as to where to go next. This might entail a change of career, moving home, starting a course, etc.

Others have specific problems, for instance connected with relationships or health. Depending on whether the astrologer is qualified to give such counselling, the consultation, or a series of

consultations, may help pinpoint the issues and point to a resolution. Some astrologers are qualified in other disciplines, for instance counselling, career counselling, financial advice, psychotherapy, herbalism, etc., and combine both successfully in their practice.

Some people simply seek a forecast for the future, whilst others would like to know the most propitious date to start a project. Those in business may seek advice, for instance on the kind of issues their business is likely to face in the near future, or on any problems that might arise in a partnership.

During a consultation in which the focus is on the natal horoscope, the astrologer aims to explore its dynamics with the client. After giving an overview of the birthchart, the astrologer will seek to find out how particular elements of it actually manifest in the client's life, i.e. what a particular planet or aspect means *to them*.

For instance, one person's Sun in Gemini may manifest as a love of writing, another's as a love of meeting and exchanging ideas with people. Another may have a particular interest in cars or some other form of travel. The consultation comes alive when clients identify and make contact with these important parts of themselves. It is remarkable how often clients come up with stories that elucidate elements of their birthchart in ways that are delightful and unexpected.

The consultation is an opportunity for clients to actively engage in the astrological story of their lives, experiencing themselves from a fresh and creative perspective.

Some astrologers will make predictions and do forecasts for clients. Others take the attitude that it is best to talk about current circumstances only, discussing how one arrived at this point, and what challenges or opportunities relating to the current situation await the client in the near future.

A skilled astrologer will make it clear that a variety of outcomes is possible depending on the choices the client makes. The forecast merely sets out when such choices are likely to be necessary and what they are likely to involve.

5 ḢOW TO CAST A ḢOROSCOPE

Thanks to recent advances in technology there are now three different ways of casting a horoscope, each with its own advantages and disadvantages.

Each method of casting a horoscope relies on knowing three items of information about the subject of the birthchart:

- date of birth
- time of birth
- place of birth

The more exactly we know the time of birth, the more accurate the horoscope will be, especially the Ascendant, and therefore each of the twelve Houses. In some countries, the time of birth is written on the birth certificate. A difference of four minutes will be reflected in a difference of approximately 1 degree to the Ascendant.

Unfortunately, such is the nature of birth, that if an accurate record is not made immediately, it can be difficult for parents to remember the exact time of the event, in which case the birthchart will need to be *rectified* (see below). For most purposes a birth time that is accurate to within 10 minutes is acceptable.

Ṫḣe astrologer's toolkit

Further information about the resources needed for casting a horoscope using each of the methods outlined below is given in Appendix 1.

Casting a horoscope by hand

For this, you will need the following items:

- An ephemeris (tables of daily planetary positions set for either midnight or noon).
- A table of Houses (used to calculate the Ascendant and Houses for a given latitude).
- An atlas or gazetteer (in order to ascertain the geographical latitude and longitude of the birthplace). A map will also suffice, although if you intend to cast birthcharts for people, you will find a good gazetteer indispensable.
- A directory of time changes, unless your gazetteer includes time-change information. This enables you to convert the local time of birth to Greenwich Mean Time (GMT) by giving the standard time zones for different countries. The tables also give the dates when clocks 'go forward' and backward, usually in the spring and autumn, at the beginning and end of Daylight Savings Time (or Summer Time). They also give any other variations such as War Time and Double Summer Time.
- A calculator.
- Pen or pencil, red and green pen, coloured felt-tip pens (optional).
- Ruler or straight edge.

Advantages

- You will develop a better understanding of how a horoscope is constructed.
- The act of drawing up a birthchart by hand is a creative act that stimulates the intuition and encourages insight.
- It is relatively inexpensive.
- It is easily portable, in the sense that you can take an ephemeris around with you – a must if you want to find out which current influences are affecting you or your friends!

Disadvantages

- You need to learn how to perform the calculations.
- It takes more time.

Using astrological software

Thanks to the decrease in cost and increase in power of personal computers in recent years, they have become ever more popular with individuals and families. At the same time, increasingly sophisticated astrology software has become available, enabling anyone with an interest in the subject to draw up horoscopes and even read interpretations without having to do the calculations by hand. Many software applications contain extensive gazetteers and accurate time change information, so you only need to input the birth data and the computer will draw up the horoscope for you. A whole plethora of advanced astrology techniques have also been made easier, more accessible and quicker to do, thanks to the astrological and programing skills of a pioneer such as Michael Erlewine of Matrix Software. In the 1970s, he was one of the first astrologers to create an astrological computer program.

There are some software packages that are either 'freeware' or 'shareware'. Freeware means that it is free to download from the Internet or copy from disk. Shareware means that you can 'try before you buy.' If you use a shareware program for more than a few weeks, or more than a set number of times, you are under a moral obligation to pay the author (usually a small fee).

Advantages

- Speed – chart calculation can be done in seconds.
- Accuracy – good quality software makes it harder to make mistakes.

- Flexibility – there are usually many different options available to suit your own level of astrological development.

Disadvantages

- Good quality software can be relatively expensive, particularly if you do not already own a computer.
- It is not portable (even 'portable' computers are often bulky and astrological software is not yet available for palmtop computers).
- Computers can, if we let them, encourage us to live in a world of abstract and ultimately meaningless information, rather than inspire us to develop our senses and intuition in our encounter with everyday life.

The Internet

A new phenomenon allied to the development of the Internet and in particular the World Wide Web, is that there are now 'web sites' at which you can input birth data and have a horoscope calculated and displayed for you, which you can then print out or save to disk. In some cases, this service is entirely free of charge (apart from the usual costs of being on the Internet). This makes astrology even more accessible and easy to experiment with.

Advantages

- Inexpensive if you already have access to the Internet.
- Ideal for occasional casting of horoscopes.

Disadvantages

- Requires a computer with a connection to the Internet.
- Lacks the more sophisticated options found in commercial software (at present).

How to cast a horoscope by hand

The aim of this section is to show, using a series of steps, how to determine the exact positions of the planets and House cusps for a given time and place of birth. Once you have these, you can enter them on to a blank chartwheel. You can then draw in the aspects (see Chapter 2) and you will have drawn up your first complete birthchart.

We will use the birthchart of Jimi Hendrix, illustrated in Chapter 2, as an example throughout and towards the end of this section are worksheets that you can photocopy and use for your own calculations.

If you wish, you can use the *Sidereal Time Worksheet* straight away (use the *Midnight Worksheet* if you are using a Midnight ephemeris) and refer to the steps below for guidance.

Notation

Be aware that zodiacal longitude, geographical latitude and longitude, and time use similar notation, which can sometimes be confusing to the beginner and more experienced astrologer alike!

Zodiacal longitude (the positions of planets or points on the horoscope in relation to the signs of the zodiac) is marked in degrees (°), minutes (') and seconds ("). Remember that each zodiac sign occupies 30°, so planets can be anywhere between 0°00'00" and 29°59'59" of a sign.

Geographical latitude and longitude (as on maps and in gazetteers) is also shown using degrees (°), minutes (') and seconds (").

Time is usually shown using hours (hr), minutes (') and seconds (").

Please be aware also that some of the calculations below involve adding or deducting periods of time. Remember that there are 24 hours in a day, 60 minutes in an hour and 60 seconds in a minute.

Checking the birth data

The first step is to make a note the subject's birth data.

1 The subject's name

1	Name	**Jimi Hendrix**

2 Sex (male or female)

2	Sex (M or F)	**M**

3 Place of birth

Note the town or city, region and country. If the subject was born somewhere obscure, it may be necessary to ask for the nearest town or city. Ideally, the place of birth will be accurate to within 2 miles/ 3 kilometres.

3	Place of birth	**Seattle, Washington, USA**

4 Latitude of birthplace

You can find the geographical latitude (degrees and minutes North or South of the equator) in your atlas or gazetteer or by looking at a map of the area.

4	Latitude (°,′ N or S)	**47°N36′**

5 Longitude of birthplace

This is the geographical longitude (degrees and minutes West or East of Greenwich, London) of the place of birth, which you can find in the same way as the latitude, above.

5	Latitude (°,′ E or W)	**122°W20′**

6 Date of birth

Note that in the United States, dates are written mm/dd/yr, whereas in Europe and elsewhere the same date is written dd/mm/yr. For example, 4/12/98 (4 December 1998) is expressed as 12/4/98 in the United States, so be sure you know which is the day of birth and which is the month.

			Day	Month	Year
6	Date of birth		27	11	1942

7 Reported time of birth

This is the time of birth, as given by the subject or obtained from parents, medical records, etc. Check that you have the correct details. In particular, make sure you know whether the time of birth was before noon (a.m.) or after noon (p.m.). Write the birth time using the 24-hour clock (e.g. 2 p.m. becomes 14hr 00'00").

			Hour	Min	Sec
7	Reported time of birth (24-hour clock)		10	15	00

UNKNOWN TIME OF BIRTH

When the exact time of birth is unknown, for instance when the subject was born 'between 3 and 4 p.m.', an astrological technique known as *rectification* may be used to determine the correct birth time.

This advanced technique is beyond the scope of this book to discuss in detail. If you want to cast a horoscope for a person whose birth time is unknown, or only vaguely known, you are advised to consult an experienced astrologer who will ask for the dates and nature of significant events in the subject's life. Transits and progressions of the subject's birthchart will then be drawn up for those dates. If the transits and progressions imply that events of that nature would

have happened at those times, the chances are that the birth time is correct. If not, different birth times are tested, until the birthchart as a whole 'clicks' into place. The subject's appearance can also be taken into account, as the Ascendant's sign and any planets in aspect to it will influence this.

Calculating the Greenwich Mean Time of Birth

Having got your birth data, you now need to convert the **reported time of birth** (i.e. the time of birth the subject gave) to *Greenwich Mean Time (GMT)*. This is because your ephemeris lists the positions of the planets at **noon GMT** each day (or midnight if you have a midnight ephemeris).

Firstly, a reminder of the reported time of birth:

			Hour	Min	Sec
7	Reported time of birth (24-hour clock)		10	15	00

The International Atlas and *The American Atlas* gazetteers (see Appendix 1) combine the information on time zones and Daylight Savings Time (below), in which case you leave steps 8 and 9 blank and fill in step 10 only. However, for the purposes of our example, we have shown both steps separately.

8 Time zone

Because **standard time zones** are different across the world, the reported time of birth is often quite different from the GMT time of birth. For instance, when it is 10:24 a.m. in London, it is 8:24 p.m. in Sydney, Australia and 2:24 a.m. in San Francisco, USA.

Depending on which of the standard time zones the birthplace was located, a certain amount of time will, therefore, need to be deducted

from, or added to, the reported time of birth. They are usually (though not always) whole hours rather than hours and minutes.

If the time zone of the birthplace is **East** of Greenwich, you will be **deducting** the appropriate amount of hours from the reported birth time, so you would enter a minus sign before the time zone difference.

If the time zone of the birthplace was **West** of Greenwich, you will be **adding** the appropriate amount of hours to the reported birth time, so you would enter a plus sign before the time zone difference.

If born in Britain or some West African countries, where Greenwich Mean Time is used, there is no need to add or deduct any time from the reported birth time (unless Daylight Savings Time was in operation, see below).

Be careful to check individual variations for the country of birth, as they can make a considerable difference to your calculations. For example, from 2:00 a.m. on 18 February 1968 to 3:00 a.m. on 31 October 1971, Britain 'changed time zones' to 15° East of Greenwich. One hour must be deducted from the reported time of birth if the subject was born in Britain during this period, even during the winter months.

In our example, Jimi Hendrix was born in Seattle, Washington, USA. (Washington State is on the west coast of the continent) which is in the Pacific Time Zone, 8 hours **West** of Greenwich. Because of this, we will be **adding** 8 hours to the reported birth time.

			Hour	Min	Sec
8	Time zone	(E –) (W +)	+8	00	00

9 Daylight Savings Time

Many countries regularly 'move their clocks forward' at certain times of the year, usually adding 1 hour to their **standard time**, and then back again later in the year. This is called **Daylight Savings Time**, or **Summer Time**.

In some countries, **War Time** has also been used, for instance during the Second World War. Then, the clocks stayed an hour ahead of standard time for a much longer period than usual.

For example, in the UK, the 'clocks went forward' by 1 hour on 10 January 1941 and stayed forward until 7 October 1946. In addition, during the summers of that period, the clocks went forward a further hour. This was called **Double Summer Time**, and you will need to check your gazetteer or time change directory carefully for the dates on which these changes occurred. As an example of this, for someone born on 1 June 1944 in London, you would need to deduct 2 hours from their reported birth time.

So, to convert the reported time of birth to GMT, simply check your directory of time changes or your gazetteer for the birthplace and date in question.

War Time was in operation in the United States from 1942 to 1945, so in our example we **deduct** 1 hour.

			Hour	Min	Sec
9	Daylight Savings Time	(–1 or 2 hours)	–1	00	00

10 Time zone and Daylight Savings Time (DST) combined

We now add steps 8 and 9 together. Alternatively, if our gazetteer or directory of time changes gives the time zone and time change information in one step, we can ignore steps 8 and 9 above and put the combined time difference in the box below, using a plus or minus sign as appropriate.

In our example, step 8 is +8 hours. We then subtract 1 hour (as step 9 is a minus number), which gives a result of +7hr 00′ 00″ (+7 hours).

			Hour	Min	Sec
10	Time zone and DST combined	=	+7	00	00

11 GMT time of birth

If step 10 has resulted in a positive (plus) number, we add this to the reported birth time (step 7). If it is a negative (minus) number, we deduct it from the reported birth time, to arrive at the GMT time of birth.

Note: For some birth times you will need to hold a picture of a clock in your mind's eye whilst performing the above calculation. For example, if you add 9 hours to a reported birth time of 22hr30'00" (i.e. 10:30 p.m.), the result will be 07hr30'00" the following morning, in which case you would write 07 30 00 in the box below. To give another example, if you had to subtract 6 hours from a reported birth time of 03hr10'00" (i.e. 3:00 a.m.), the result would be 21hr10'00" (i.e. 9:10 p.m. the previous night).

In our example, we add 7 hours to Jimi's reported birth time of 10hr15'00" to arrive at 17hr15'00".

			Hour	Min	Sec
11	GMT time of birth	=	17	15	00

12 GMT date of birth

Usually, the GMT date of birth is the same as the reported date of birth. However, if, in performing step 11 above, the resultant time was after 24hr00'00" (see note, above) then the GMT date of birth is the day **after** the reported date of birth. If the resultant time is before 00hr00'00", then the GMT date of birth is the day **before** the reported date of birth.

In our example, Jimi's GMT date of birth is the same as his reported date of birth.

			Day	Month	Year
12	GMT date of birth		27	11	1942

Congratulations! You now have the GMT time and date of birth. Using your ephemeris, you will later use these two pieces of information to determine the exact positions of the planets. Firstly however, we have a few more calculations to do, but you will soon be in a position to start drawing up a birthchart, starting with the House cusps and the signs of the zodiac.

Calculating the Sidereal Time of Birth

To work out the positions of the Ascendant, Midheaven and the House cusps, we need to know the exact *Sidereal Time*, or 'star time', of birth. This is because tables of Houses list the positions of the House cusps for given Sidereal Times. We must, therefore, convert our Greenwich Mean Time of birth to Sidereal Time. We get the Sidereal Time at noon on the GMT date of birth from our ephemeris (or midnight if we are using a midnight ephemeris), from which we can then calculate the correct Sidereal Time of birth.

Sidereal Time reflects the exact period of time for the Earth to travel around the Sun, as measured against the background of the stars.

13 Sidereal Time at noon/midnight GMT

Firstly, look in the ephemeris for the correct GMT date of birth (step 12, above) and write down the Sidereal Time shown for that day. This will be the Sidereal Time for noon GMT if using a noon ephemeris, or midnight GMT if using a midnight ephemeris.

		Hour	Min	Sec
13	Sidereal Time at noon/midnight GMT (Use correct GMT date, as above)	16	23	4

14 Interval between GMT time of birth and noon

Now work out the **interval** (difference in time) in hours, minutes (and seconds if necessary), between the GMT time of birth and GMT noon. If the GMT time of birth is **before noon**, put a **minus (–)** symbol in front of the time. If the GMT time of birth is **after noon**, put a **plus (+)** symbol in front of the time. This is because we will later deduct or add this amount of time from the Sidereal Time at noon/midnight (step 16).

If using a midnight ephemeris, use a plus symbol, because you will be adding that amount of time to the Sidereal Time at midnight (00hrs).

For instance, say we are using a noon ephemeris, and we are casting a birthchart for someone with a GMT time of birth of 3hr41'00" (03:41 a.m.). The Interval between 03:41 a.m. and noon is 8 hours and 19 minutes, so we would write –08 19 00 in the box below. If we were using a midnight ephemeris, we would write +03 41 00.

In the example we are using, however, Jimi Hendrix's GMT time of birth (step 11, above) is 17hr15'00" (5:15 p.m.), so we write +05 15 00.

			Hour	Min	Sec
14	Interval between GMT time of birth (step 11) and noon GMT	(a.m. –) (p.m. +)	+05	15	00

15 Acceleration on the Interval

Since a sidereal day is not 24 hours but 23 hours' 56 minutes 4 seconds, we must take account of this in our calculations. To do this, we **deduct (or add) 10 seconds for every hour, or 1 second for every 6 minutes** of the above Interval. This is called the 'Acceleration on the Interval'. Round up to the nearest second if necessary.

If the Interval (step 14, above) is a positive number (i.e. the GMT time of birth is after noon), the Acceleration on the Interval will also be a positive number, and we will later add it to the Sidereal Time at noon, along with the Interval.

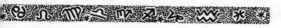

Likewise, if the Interval is a negative number (i.e. the GMT time of birth is before noon), the Acceleration will also be negative and we will, therefore, later (step 16) deduct it from the Sidereal Time at noon, along with the Interval.

In our example, the Interval is +05hr15'00", so the Acceleration is +00hr00'53" (i.e. 53 seconds).

			Hour	Min	Sec
15	Acceleration on Interval (10" per hour)	(a.m. –) (p.m. +)	+00	00	53

16 Sidereal Time of birth at Greenwich

Now we simply deduct the Interval (step 14) and the Acceleration on the Interval (step 15) from the Sidereal Time at noon if they are both negative numbers, or add them if they are both positive.

In our example, the Sidereal Time at noon is 16hr23'04". To this we *add* (because the GMT time of birth is after noon) the Interval, which is 05hr15'00", then the Acceleration on the Interval, which is 00hr00'53". The result is 21hr38'57". This is the **Sidereal Time of birth at Greenwich**.

			Hour	Min	Sec
16	Sidereal Time of birth at Greenwich i.e. if a.m. 13–14–15. If p.m. 13+14+15	=	21	38	57

17 Longitude Equivalent

To take account of the longitude of birth (degrees and minutes East or West of Greenwich), **for every degree** of longitude **East of 0°, add 4 minutes** to the above figure, or **for every degree West of 0°, deduct 4 minutes**. This is called the Longitude Equivalent. Unlike the Acceleration on the Interval, this step can make a significant difference to the resulting Sidereal Time, so check your figures carefully at this stage.

Most locations are not exactly whole degrees from Greenwich so, to aid calculation, 1 minute of longitude corresponds to 4 seconds of time, whilst 15 degrees of longitude corresponds to 1 hour of time.

Note that the addition or subtraction you do at this stage is the opposite of what you did in step 8 above.

Using our example, Jimi Hendrix was born in Seattle, Washington, on the West Coast of the United States, the longitude for which is **122°W20'** (step 5, above). This gives us a Longitude Equivalent of 489'20" (489 minutes and 20 seconds of time), or 8 hours, 9 minutes and 20 seconds. Because Seattle is West of Greenwich, this figure will be deducted from the Sidereal Time at Greenwich (step 16, above), so we put a minus sign before it.

			Hour	Min	Sec
17	Longitude Equivalent (add 4' per 1° East, or deduct 4' per 1° West)	(E +) (W –)	–8	9	20

18 Sidereal Time of birth

Finally, add the Longitude Equivalent (step 17) to the Sidereal Time of birth at Greenwich (if the Longitude Equivalent is a positive number), or deduct it if it is a negative number. If the final figure is greater than 24 hours, deduct 24 hours.

In our example, we deduct 8 hours, 9 minutes and 20 seconds from 21 hours 38 minutes and 57 seconds to get a Sidereal Time of 13 hours, 29 minutes and 37 seconds.

			Hour	Min	Sec
18	**Sidereal Time of birth** i.e. add or deduct 16 to or from 17 (subtract 12 hrs if greater than 24 hrs)	=	13	29	37

Congratulations! You now have the Sidereal Time of birth, which you will be able to use to determine the House cusps, using your table of Houses.

sidereal time worksheet for a noon ephemeris

Use the worksheets below when drawing up birthcharts.

1	Name	
2	Sex (M or F)	
3	Place of birth	
4	Latitude (°, ′ , ″ N or S)	
5	Longitude (°, ′, ″ E or W)	

		Day	Month	Year
6	Date of birth			

			Hour	Min	Sec
7	Reported time of birth (24-hour clock)				
8	Time zone*	(E −, W +)			
9	Daylight Savings Time (DST)*	(− 1 or 2 hours)			
10	Time zone and DST combined				
11	GMT time of birth (step 7 plus or minus step 10)	=			

		Day	Month	Year
12	GMT date of birth			

			Hour	Min	Sec
13	Sidereal Time at noon GMT (Use correct GMT date of birth)				
14	Interval between GMT time of birth (step 11) and noon GMT	(a.m. −) (p.m. +)			
15	Acceleration (10 secs per hour)	(a.m. −) (p.m. +)			
16	Sidereal Time of birth at Greenwich i.e. if a.m: 13−14−15. If p.m: 13+14+15	=			
17	Longitude Equivalent (add 4 mins per 1° East, or deduct 4 mins per 1° West)	(E +) (W −)			
18	**Sidereal Time of birth** i.e. 16 plus or minus 17. Subtract 24 hrs if result is greater than 24 hrs.	=			

* Remember that you can leave steps 8 and 9 blank and fill in step 10 only, if your gazetteer or time change directory combines time zone and Daylight Savings Time information.

SIDEREAL TIME WORKSHEET FOR A MIDNIGHT EPHEMERIS

1	Name				
2	Sex (M or F)				
3	Place of birth				
4	Latitude (°, ′ , ″ N or S)				
5	Longitude (°, ′ , ″ E or W)				

		Day	Month	Year
6	Date of birth			

		Hour	Min	Sec
7	Reported time of birth (24-hour clock)			
8	Time zone* (E –, W +)			
9	Daylight Savings Time (DST)* (– 1 or 2 hours)			
10	Time zone and DST combined			
11	GMT time of birth (step 7 plus or minus step 10) =			

		Day	Month	Year
12	GMT date of birth			

		Hour	Min	Sec
13	Sidereal Time at midnight (00hr) GMT (Use correct GMT date of birth)			
14	Interval between midnight GMT (0hr) and GMT time of birth (step 11) (+)			
15	Acceleration (10 secs per hour) (+)			
16	Sidereal Time of birth at Greenwich i.e. 13+14+15 =			
17	Longitude Equivalent (add 4 mins per 1° East, or deduct 4 mins per 1° West) (E +) (W –)			
18	**Sidereal Time of birth** i.e. 16 plus or minus 17. Subtract 24 hrs if result is greater than 24 hrs. =			

* Remember that you can leave steps 8 and 9 blank and fill in step 10 only, if your gazetteer or time change directory combines time zone and Daylight Savings Time information.

Calculating the House cusps

For this, you need a table of Houses for the given latitude of birth.

how to read a table of houses

Below is a section from a typical table of Houses, for latitude 47° N 29′, the closest given latitude to the Seattle birthplace of Jimi Hendrix.

	Sid. Time	10 (X)	11 (XI)	12 (XII)	ASC (I)	2 (II)	3 (III)
		♎	♏	♐	♐	♒	♓
	H M S	°	°	°	° ′	°	°
A)	13 28′ 52″	24	18	7	24 37	5	20
B)	13 32′ 38″	25	19	8	25 26	6	21

Section of table of Houses for latitude 47° N 29′

Sidereal Times are given on the left-hand column. The next column shows the positions (in degrees of zodiacal longitude) of the Xth House cusp (MC) for each Sidereal Time. The next two columns show the XIth House cusp and the XIIth cusp. The fifth column shows the Ist House cusp (Asc), in degrees and minutes, for greater accuracy. The last two show the IInd and IIIrd House cusps.

We draw these cusps on a blank chartwheel, starting with the Asc which by convention we will draw on the left-hand side.

The IVth, Vth, VIth, VIIth, VIIIth and IXth House cusps are always directly opposite the Xth (MC), XIth XIIth, Ist (Asc), IInd and IIIrd respectively, so can be calculated easily. For example, if the Asc is 24° 37′ Sagittarius, the VIIth House cusp will be 24° 37′ Gemini.

finding the house cusps

The easiest way to calculate the House cusps is simply to look in the table of Houses for the latitude closest to the latitude of the

birthplace. Then look up the Sidereal Time closest to the Sidereal Time of birth that you previously calculated in steps 1–18 above. On the same line, you will find the cusps of the MC, XIth, XIIth, Asc, IInd and IIIrd House cusps.

Since the Sidereal Time of 13hr28'52" in the table of Houses above is closest to Jimi Hendrix's exact Sidereal Time of 13hr29'37", the House cusps shown in row A, above are used.

The cusps of the opposing Houses are therefore:

4 (IV)	5 (V)	6 (VI)	7 (VII)	8 (VIII)	9 (IX)
24 ♈	18 ♉	7 ♊	24 37 ♊	5 ♋	20 ♍

Given that most reported birth times have at least a five-minute margin of error, following the procedure above is usually sufficient and you can always fine-tune your results later (see below).

Congratulations! You have determined the Asc, MC and House cusps, and can now draw them on to a blank chartwheel.

Using a Northern Hemisphere table of Houses for a Southern Hemisphere birth

If you have a table of Houses for the Northern Hemisphere, but the subject was born south of the equator, you can still work out the House cusps. Simply add 12 hours to the Sidereal Time of birth (if the result is then greater than 24 hours, subtract 24 hours). Using this Southern Hemisphere Sidereal Time, look up the House cusps in the same way as before, reading the table corresponding to the correct latitude (except that you are using the equivalent Northern latitude). For example, if born in Sydney (latitude 33°S52'), look up the nearest latitude to 33°N52'.

Finally, reverse all the House cusp signs so that they are directly opposite to those listed in the table of Houses. Thus 4° Aries becomes 4° Libra, and so on.

Calculating the Ascendant and Midheaven exactly (optional)

If either the Ascendant or Midheaven is close to a sign cusp, or if you know the exact birth time, it is worth determining their positions more closely. It is also worthwhile if you intend to experiment with Progressed charts or look at transits to the Asc and MC.

When the Sidereal Time (and hence the House cusps) listed in the table of Houses do not exactly match your own Sidereal Time of birth, obviously the exact House cusp positions are also 'somewhere in-between' the two nearest Sidereal Times shown.

The diagram below shows what you are aiming to find out:

	Sidereal Time	10 (X)	ASC (I)
Previous closest in TOH	13 28′ 52″	24	24 37
Exact ST of birth	13 29′ 37″	?	?
Following closest TOH	13 32′ 38″	25	25 26

Essentially, you need to determine the difference between the closest preceding Sidereal Time listed in the table of Houses and the exact Sidereal Time of birth (as previously determined in steps 1–18 above). Then you can apply the same **proportional difference** to the positions of the Asc and MC as listed in the table of Houses.

Because the intervening House cusps listed in most tables of Houses are only accurate to within half a degree, they should be taken directly from the table for the closest Sidereal Time.

Compensating for an Unlisted Birthplace Latitude

Since some tables of Houses list House positions at approximately 1.5° increments of latitude, if the birthplace is not very close to this latitude the Asc and MC may be several minutes out. Therefore, we have to begin our calculations by compensating for this difference.

To illustrate this point, here is the section of the table of Houses for the previous closest latitude to our example birthplace of Seattle, USA.

	Sid. Time	10 (X)	11 (XI)	12 (XII)	ASC (I)	2 (II)	3 (III)
		♎	♏	♐	♐	♒	♓
	H M S	°	°	°	° ′	°	°
A)	13 28′ 52″	24	18	7	24 37	5	20
B)	13 32′ 38″	25	19	8	25 26	6	21

Section of table of Houses for latitude 47° N 29′

Below is a section from the next page of the table of Houses, showing the data for 48° N 14′, the following closest latitude to Seattle. Since Seattle is situated at 47° N 36′, the House cusps we are looking for are going to be 'somewhere in between' those listed on each page.

	Sid. Time	10 (X)	11 (XI)	12 (XII)	ASC (I)	2 (II)	3 (III)
		♎	♏	♐	♐	♒	♓
	H M S	°	°	°	° ′	°	°
A)	13 28′ 52″	24	18	7	23 55	5	20
B)	13 32′ 38″	25	19	7	24 44	6	21

Section of table of Houses for latitude 49° N 14′

The MC positions remain the same for both latitudes, but the Asc is different at each of the two latitudes, therefore we need to find some way of calculating what the Asc is at the exact latitude of Seattle.

ascendant calculation worksɓeet

The following steps, *a* to *v*, enable us to find out the exact
Ascendant and Midheaven. The figures used in bold are from our
example chart.

The first section, rows *a* to *j*, enable us to adjust the results of our
calculations to compensate for the difference between the exact
latitude of birth and the latitudes shown in the table of Houses. If
the birthplace latitude is the same as one shown in our table of
Houses, we can ignore these steps and start at step *k*.

	Geographic latitude:	Deg	Min	Sec
a	Previous closest latitude in TOH	47	29	
b	Next closest latitude in TOH	48	14	
c	*b* minus *a* in minutes		45	
d	Exact latitude of birthplace (to nearest minute)	47	36	
e	*d* minus *a* in minutes		07	
f	*e* divided by *c* (proportional difference)		0.155	
	Zodiacal longitude:	Deg	Min	Sec
g	Previous closest Asc in TOH for previous closest latitude	24	37	
h	Previous closest Asc in TOH for next closest latitude	23	55	
i	*g* minus *h* in minutes		42	
j	*i* multiplied by *f*, to nearest minute		7	

Row *j* above represents the difference in minutes of zodiacal longitude
that you will later subtract from or add to the Ascendant position
calculated in step *u* below, in order to compensate for the exact latitude
of the birthplace. **Subtract** if the Asc is decreasing in longitude from
one page of the table of Houses to the next, and **add** if it is increasing.

Time:	Hr	Min	Sec
k	Exact Sidereal Time of birth (as calculated previously)	13	29	37
l	Previous closest Sidereal Time in TOH	13	28	52
m	Following closest Sidereal Time in TOH	13	32	38
n	m minus l (in seconds) =			226
o	k minus l (in seconds) =			45
p	o divided by n (proportional difference)		0.2	

Zodiacal longitude:	Deg	Min	Sec
q	Previous closest Asc in TOH (as in g)	24	37	00
r	Next closest Ascendant	25	26	
s	r minus q (in minutes) =		49	
t	p × s (to nearest minute) =		10	
u	**Ascendant** i.e. q + t =	24	47	00
v	**Corrected Ascendant** i.e. u − j =	24	40	00

The correct Ascendant is thus 24° ♐ 40′. In fact, the Ascendant as calculated by computer is 24° ♐ 41′. The one-minute difference reflects our rounding up or down to the nearest minute to make calculation easier, but the degree of precision we have achieved is perfectly acceptable.

To calculate the exact position of the Midheaven, substitute the Midheaven positions in rows g, h, q and r.

Remember that if you are using a table of Houses for Northern latitudes for a Southern latitude birthplace, add 12 hours to the Sidereal Time and then reverse the resultant Houses cusp signs, so that Pisces becomes Virgo, etc.

blank ascendant/midheaven calculation sheet

	Geographic latitude:	Deg	Min	Sec
a	Previous closest latitude in TOH			
b	Next closest latitude in TOH			
c	b minus a in minutes			
d	Exact latitude of birthplace (to nearest minute)			
e	d minus a in minutes			
f	e divided by c (proportional difference)			

	Zodiacal longitude:	Deg	Min	Sec
g	Previous closest Asc in TOH for previous closest latitude			
h	Previous closest Asc in TOH for next closest latitude			
i	Difference between g and h (in minutes)			
j	i multiplied by f, to nearest minute			

	Time:	Hr	Min	Sec
k	Exact Sidereal Time of birth (as calculated previously in step 18 above)*			
l	Previous closest Sidereal Time in TOH*			
m	Following closest Sidereal Time in TOH*			
n	m minus l (in seconds) =			
o	k minus l (in seconds) =			
p	o divided by n (proportional difference)			

	Zodiacal longitude:	Deg	Min	Sec
q	Previous closest Asc in TOH (same as g, above)			
r	Next closest Asc in TOH			
s	r minus q (in minutes) =			
t	p × s (to nearest minute) =			
u	**Ascendant** i.e. q + t =			
v	**Corrected Ascendant** i.e. u plus or minus j =			

* Remember to use corrected Sidereal Time if birthplace is South of the equator.
To check your result, remember that the exact Ascendant will fall between the closest
Ascendants shown in the table of Houses and there will be a small correction for the
correct latitude.

Drawing the birthchart

You can now begin drawing up the birthchart. Copy the blank chart below (Figure 12), or draw it using compasses and a straight edge. Leave out the 360 degree markers if you wish, but to help orient yourself when drawing the House cusps and planets, draw in marker points every 5 degrees.

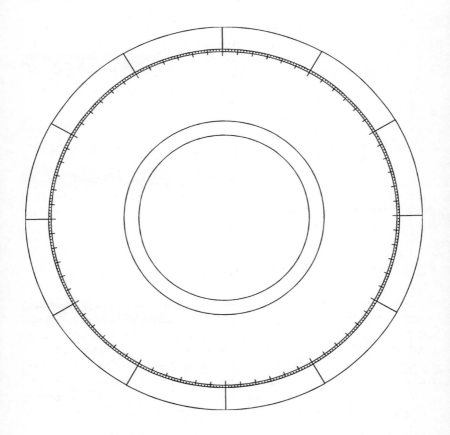

Figure 12 Blank chartwheel

Drawing in the Ascendant

Now you know your House cusps, you can start filling in the blank chartwheel. Refer to Figures 5 and 6 in Chapter 2 to help you. Start with the Ascendant, by drawing a straight line at the appropriate degree position of either of the two left-most blank zodiac signs. If your Ascendant is greater than 15°, draw the line in the upper 30° segment. If it is less than 15°, draw it in the lower 30° segment. This is simply because, by convention, the Ascendant is always shown on the left of the birthchart. Remember that you read a horoscope anticlockwise. Draw the line across the centre of the chartwheel as in Figure 5, and write the position in degrees (and minutes if applicable) on the outside of the birthchart. Mark the Ascendant with its glyph '(Asc)' and an arrowhead, so that you can see this important point at a glance.

Drawing the zodiac sign glyphs

Since you know which sign of the zodiac your Asc is located, you can draw in the glyph for that sign as well as the 11 other signs, in the outer ring of the birthchart, following the correct order anticlockwise around the chartwheel (see Figure 2).

Completing the House cusps

Next, draw the cusps of the IInd and its opposite, the VIIIth House, then the IIIrd and its opposite, the IXth House. If you are reading the positions direct from the table of Houses, draw the cusp of the Xth House (Midheaven) next (which will be near the top of the chartwheel) together with its opposite cusp, that of the IVth House. Mark the Midheaven with its glyph, MC, and an arrowhead. Then the cusp of the XIth House and its opposite, the Vth, and lastly the cusp of the XIIth House, and its opposite, the VIth.

Now you can mark which House is which by entering the appropriate roman numerals I to XII on the inner circle, as in Figure 5.

Congratulations! You have now marked the House cusps on to the birthchart! You also know the Ascendant (or Rising Sign), the Midheaven, and where each House begins and ends.

The next step is to add the planets, but first, you will need to calculate their positions.

Calculating the planets' positions

For this stage, you need your ephemeris and possibly a calculator.

How to read an ephemeris

Before we begin, we need to know how to read an ephemeris. Below is a section of a typical noon ephemeris, showing data for Friday 27 November 1942 and Saturday 28, the following day. Note that for reasons of space, the positions of Saturn, Uranus, Neptune and Pluto have been omitted.

Day	Sid. Time	☉	☽	True ☊	☿	♀	♂	♃
27F	16 23′ 04″	4° ♐ 36′49″	25° ♋ 29′ 56″	28° ♌ ℞ 44.9′	2° ♐ 36.2′	7° ♐ 19.5′	17° ♏ 22.4′	24°℞ ♋ 52.2′
28 Sa	16 27′ 1″	5° 37′ 33″	7° ♌ 18′ 42″	28° 41.0′	4° 10.8	8° 34.9′	18° 3.7′	24° 4932′

Noon ephemeris for 27 and 28 November 1942

Each row lists the positions of the planets at noon each day. (A midnight ephemeris lists the positions of the planets at 00hr.) Some noon ephemerides also list the midnight positions of the Moon.

The left-most column usually shows the date and day of the week. The second column shows the Sidereal Time at noon, or at midnight in a midnight ephemeris. Sometimes the minutes and seconds symbols are left out and only the numbers given.

In the example above, the third to the seventh columns show the positions of the planets in zodiacal longitude, i.e. degrees and minutes, from 00°00′ to 29°59′ of each sign. The glyph for the zodiac sign is shown at the top of each monthly table and again when a planet has changed sign. In the above example, the Moon is near the end of Cancer at noon on 27 November, so the glyph for Cancer (♋) is shown in the Moon's column for that day. It enters Leo a few hours later the same day and by noon the following day it is at 7° 18′ 42″ Leo, so the glyph for Leo (♌) is shown on 28 November.

Note that in some ephemerides, the Sun and Moon's positions are shown in degrees, minutes and seconds, whilst the other planets' positions are shown in degrees and minutes, with the seconds being shown as a decimal fraction of a minute (so 0.5′ is equal to 30 seconds). This may seem confusing but, in practice, accuracy of 1′ of arc is more than acceptable, so we can round the seconds up or down to the nearest minute.

Note also that in the above example, the Moon's Node (your ephemeris might call it True ☊) is retrograde (℞), as is Jupiter.

To find out which sign (and whereabouts in the sign) each planet was located for a given GMT date and time of birth, simply look in your ephemeris at the **correct GMT date of birth**.

If you are lucky enough to be dealing with a noon GMT time of birth, you can read the planets' positions directly from the ephemeris at the appropriate date. However, the chances are that the GMT time of birth is not noon, in which case some calculations are required in order to ascertain the positions exactly.

Doing the calculations

To work out the positions of the planets to within half a degree, which is acceptable when you are first learning to cast horoscopes, you can almost read them directly from the ephemeris for the appropriate GMT date of birth, with the exception of the Sun, Moon, Mercury and Venus.

As we have seen, the Sun moves approximately 1° per day, whilst the Moon moves on average 13°, or approximately 1° every two hours. Mercury rarely moves more than 2° per day, whilst Venus rarely moves more than 1°30' per day. The Moon's Node, Mars, Jupiter, Saturn, Uranus, Neptune and Pluto move less than 1° per day.

To calculate the exact positions of the planets, use the **Table of Proportional Logarithms for Finding the Planets' Places** (see Figure 13). Using the table avoids the need to do complex calculations that involve multiplying zodiacal longitude by fractions. Logarithms sound tricky but, as we shall discover, the table is actually simple to use.

Using the Table of Proportional Logarithms

Using the log table, you can work out how far each planet moved from its noon position in the ephemeris to the exact time of birth, and then add (or subtract) this distance to find out the exact position of the planet. This involves six simple steps. If using a midnight ephemeris, substitute 'midnight' for 'noon' in steps 1, 3 and 6.

Note that columns 2 to 15 in the Proportional Logarithm table saves space by leaving out the decimal point before each number, but this should be written in when you do your sum.

1 Calculate the **daily motion** of the planet, i.e. how many degrees and minutes of the zodiac it is travelling from noon to noon.
2 Write down the proportional log of the planet's **daily motion**, by looking in the appropriate column (corresponding to the degrees of zodiacal longitude travelled), and the appropriate row (corresponding to minutes of zodiacal longitude).
3 Write down the proportional log that corresponds to the **Interval** between the GMT time of birth and noon GMT (step 14 in the Sidereal Time Worksheet on page 99).
4 **Add** the two proportional logs together.

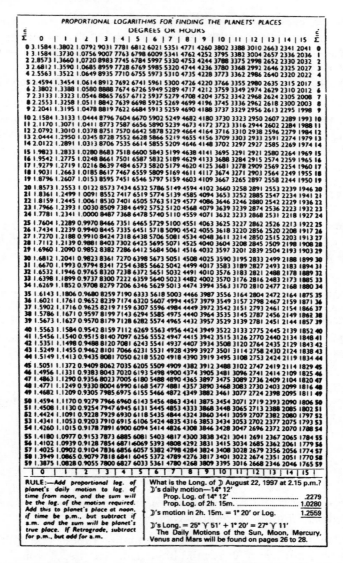

Figure 13 Table of Proportional Logarithms for Finding the Planets' Places, reproduced with kind permission from W. Foulsham & Co. Ltd (see Appendix 1).

5　Find the resulting proportional log in the log table. If necessary, find the one closest to this figure. The column it is in represents how many degrees of zodiacal longitude the planet has moved, its row represents how many minutes.

6　Add this distance to the planet's noon position if the time of birth is p.m., or subtract it if born before noon.

Note: if the planet is retrograde (i.e. moving backwards in the zodiac), do the reverse of step 6 by subtracting the distance from the planet's noon position if born after noon, or adding if born before noon.

Example

In our example chart, the Interval between noon and Jimi's GMT time of birth of 17hr15′00″ (05:15 p.m.) is 5 hours and 15 minutes. We will work out the exact position of the Moon in his birthchart.

1　We start by working out the **daily motion**. The Moon's was at 25° ♋ 30′ at noon on 27 November 1942, and 7° ♌ 19′ at noon the following day (figures rounded up to the nearest minute of arc). The Moon's daily motion was therefore **11° 49′**.

2　In the Table of Proportional Logarithms, we find that the log for 11° 49′ is **0.3077**.

3　The proportional log for the **Interval** (5hr 15′) is **0.6600**.

4　0.3077 + 0.6600 = **0.9677**.

5　Looking in the table, we find that the closest proportional log to 0.9677 is 0.9680. This corresponds to **2° 35′**.

6　Since Jimi was born after noon, we add 2° 35′ to the Moon's noon position of 25° ♋ 30′ to arrive at an exact position of **28° ♋ 05′**. The Moon was at exactly this position in the zodiac at his moment of birth.

Remember that if he had been born before noon, we would have deducted step 5 from the noon position.

Remember, too, that if we had been calculating Jupiter's position in our example birthchart, we would have deducted step 5 from Jupiter's position at noon, since Jupiter was retrograde.

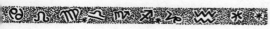

Using the above log table, we arrive at the following planetary positions for our example birthchart:

Planet	☉	☽	☊	☿	♀	♂
Position	4° ♐ 50′	28 ♋ 05′	29° ♌ ℞ 20′	2° ♐ 57′	7° ♐ 36′	17° ♏ 31′

Planet	♃	♄	♅	♆	♇
Position	24°℞ ♋ 51′	9°℞ Ⅱ 22′	2°℞ Ⅱ 28′	1° ♎ 40′	7°℞ ♌ 11′

ENTERING THE PLANETS ON THE BIRTHCHART

You can now draw the glyphs for each of the planets on to the birthchart, referring back to Figure 6 in Chapter 2 if necessary. Write their positions in degrees and minutes next to the glyph, so that you can tell at a glance exactly where they are located.

DRAWING THE ASPECTS

Having drawn the Houses and the planets, you can now work out the aspects, as per *The aspects*, Chapter 2, and add them to the birthchart.

You can also optionally enter the aspects into an 'aspect grid' like the one below. This shows the aspects for our example birthchart, together with the difference between the ideal aspect and the actual aspect.

This is optional, but helps you see at a glance the closest (and therefore the strongest) aspects in the birthchart. In the example below, Mercury is 0°29′ from being in exact opposition to Uranus, and the Ascendant is 0°29′ from being in exact sextile to the Midheaven. These are, therefore, the closest two aspects in the birthchart.

The aspect grid (planets along the diagonal: ☉, ☽, ☿, ♀, ♂, ♃, ♄, ♅, ♆, ♇, ☊, ASC, MC):

☉												
△ 6°45′	☽											
♂ 1°53′	△ 4°52′	☿										
♂ 2°46′		♂ 4°39′	♀									
	♂ 3°13′			♂								
☍ 4°32′		☍ 1°46′			♄							
☍ 2°22′	✶ 4°24′	☍ 0°29′				♅						
✶ 3°10′	✶ 3°36′	✶ 1°16′				△ 0°48′	♆					
△ 2°21′		△ 4°14′	△ 0°25′			✶ 2°11′	✶ 4°42′	♇				
	□ 3°37′						□ 0°40′		☊			
									△ 4°39′	ASC		
□ 3°53′				□ 0°39′						✶ 0°29′	MC	

ELEMENT, MODE AND POLARITY

Finally, you can work out the Element, mode, polarity and House mode of the planets in the birthchart and enter them on a grid like those below, in which the figures for our example birthchart have been entered.

Element				Mode			Polarity		House mode		
F	A	W	E	Car	Fix	Mut	+	−	Ang	Suc	Cad
5	4	3	0	4	2	6	9	3	3	4	3

Congratulations! You have now cast your first horoscope and you can interpret it using the keywords in Chapter 3.

PRACTICE

Cast your own birthchart using the worksheets in this chapter, using the blank chartwheel on page 108.

6

BEYOND NATAL ASTROLOGY

*L*ike any discipline that has evolved over thousands of years, astrology has developed its own specialisms. The focus in this book has been on natal astrology which is based on interpreting a horoscope or birthchart drawn up for the moment of a person's birth. There are many other branches, however. Some are listed below, although it is beyond the scope of this book to explain their use in detail.

FORECASTING

Transits involve looking in the ephemeris at the current positions of the planets, then relating these to a natal birthchart. The planets, as they orbit the zodiac, act as 'triggers' to planets in the birthchart, giving rise to events, relationships and all the other changes we experience in our lives. For instance, if transiting Uranus is conjuncting (i.e. crossing over) our natal Sun, it is a good time to make creative changes in our lives and do things that we would normally consider too adventurous. On the other hand, the transiting Moon, since it moves so quickly round the zodiac, has little effect, save perhaps on our day-to-day moods and feelings.

In addition to aspects to natal positions, we can also take account of which house a transiting planet is travelling through. For example, Saturn transiting the VIth House may correspond to a long period of increased work responsibilities or a heavier workload. It is a good time to take particular care of our health and avoid too much stress.

Progressions are more of a symbolic technique:

- *Secondary progressions* involve looking at the positions of the planets in the days or weeks after birth, taking one day in the ephemeris as equalling one year in the individual's life. For someone who is 20 years old, one would look at the positions of the planets 20 days after the birth date. Aspects that progressed planets make to natal positions tell us about how our lives are progressing or unfolding.

- In *solar arc progressions*, each planet is 'progressed' forward by the same distance – the distance the Sun moves in one day (approximately 1°). Using the above example, each planet would be progressed 20° forward, 1° equalling one year of life.

SYNASTRY AND COMPOSITE CHARTS

Synastry involves exploring the relationship between two people by looking at how their two birthcharts inter-relate. For instance, if one person's Saturn conjuncts another's Moon, he or she may tend to limit the Moon person's emotional expression, or find it threatening in some way. The Moon person may feel immature or overly emotional around the Saturn person, but may also feel secure, since the Saturn person provides a stable structure and may seem older and wiser. Compatible Moons, for instance if both are in Water signs, indicate that the two people could share the same home without getting irritated by each other's personal habits or emotional needs.

If you take two people's birthcharts and draw up a third chart, placing each planet at the midpoint position of the first and second charts, you create a *composite birthchart*. For example, if person A has the Sun at 5° Pisces and person B has the Sun at 15° Taurus, the composite Sun would be at 10° Aries. The composite birthchart says something about the potential of the relationship as a thing in itself (sometimes known as a *dyad*), whereas synastry is more about how person A experiences person B and vice versa.

Other techniques

Mundane astrology is the astrology of world and political events, and involves looking at the current positions of the planets to see what influences are affecting the world in general. The 'birthcharts' of individual countries can also be explored in relationship to current planetary positions.

Financial astrology can be used to track the fortunes of the stock market, currencies and individual businesses.

Horary astrology is an ancient branch of astrology concerned with divination and answers to individual questions, such as 'where is my wallet?'.

Electional astrology is used to choose the most propitious time for an event, such as the formation of a company or the date of a marriage.

Some complementary health practitioners use *medical astrology* to diagnose the likely cause, duration and treatment for an illness.

Astrogeography shows how being in different locations on Earth may affect our experiences and our fortunes.

Experiential astrology enables participants to understand astrology through the senses and imagination, for instance by creating collages of the planets and signs or expressing planetary energies through dance, music or song, visualisation or ritual.

Astrodrama similarly involves drama and role play, though has the aim of using the subject's birthchart therapeutically, to explore and perhaps resolve specific personal or interpersonal problems.

Midpoints involves looking at planets midway between two other planets, or planets sharing a common midpoint in the horoscope. These are interpreted in much the same way as aspects.

PRACTICE

Look in the ephemeris at the positions of the planets today. How do they relate to the planets in your own birthchart? Keep an astrological diary containing transits and progressions to your horoscope, and see whether they match events in your life.

APPENDIX 1

RESOURCE LIST

ASTROLOGICAL ORGANISATIONS

The Astrological Association, Lee Valley Technopark, Tottenham Hale, London N17 9LN. Tel: 0181 880 4848; Fax: 0181 880 4849.

Federation of Australian Astrologers Inc., 24 Berryman Street, North Ryde, 2113 New South Wales, Australia. E-mail: faa@peg.apc.org.

Canadian Association for Astrological Education, 4191 Stonemason Crescent, Mississauga, Ontario L5L 2Z6, Canada.

Institut Metaphysique Occidental, 836 av. Outremont, Outremont, Quebec H2V 3N6, Canada. Tel: (514) 273-7326.

Astrological Society of South Africa, PO Box 2968, Rivonia 2128, Gauteng, South Africa. Tel: +27-11-867-4153.

American Federation of Astrologers, PO Box 22040, Tempe, Arizona 85285-2040, USA. Tel: 602-838-1751; Fax: 602-838-8293.

Blank chartwheels: contact the above organisations, or your local astrology book stockist.

Ephemeris *The American Ephemeris for the 21st Century*, Neil F. Michelsen (ACS Publications Inc.); *Raphael's Annual Ephemeris* (W. Foulsham & Co. Ltd, Bennetts Close, Cippenham SL1 5AP (UK)

Table of Houses *Table of Houses for Northern Latitudes* (W. Foulsham & Co. Ltd)

Gazetteer/Time changes:

The International Atlas, Thomas Shanks (ACS Publications Inc.) – Latitudes, longitudes, time zones and time changes (except USA).

The American Atlas, Thomas Shanks (as above).

Time changes: *Time Changes in the World*, Doris Chase Douane (American Federation of Astrologers). *Time changes in the USA* (as above).

Recommended computer programs

Winstar, Matrix Software (*Windows)*.

UK: *Matrix UK*, Library Wing, Abbey St. Bathans House, Duns, Berwickshire TD11 3TX. Tel: 01361 840 340. Fax: 01361 840 284, Internet: www.astral.demon.co.uk

Australia: *Matrix Australia*, 2/6 Peace Street, Glen Iris, 3146 Victoria. Tel/Fax: 613 9885 4507.

Canada/USA: *Matrix Software*, 407 N. State, Big Rapids MI 49307. Tel: 1-616-796-3060.

Solar Fire, Astrolabe (*Windows*)

UK: *Roy Gillett Consultants*, 32 Glynswood, Camberley, Surrey GU15 1HU. Tel/Fax: 01276 683898.

Australia: *Astrolabe Australia*, 94 Blaxland Road, Wentworth Falls, 2782 New South Wales. Tel/Fax: 047 573912.

Canada/USA: *Astrolabe*, Box 1750, Brewster, MA 02631. Tel: 1 (800) 843-6682; Fax: 1 (508) 896-5289.

Miscellaneous software:

South Africa: *Rod Suskin*, 1 Fairview, 13 Chelmsford Road, Vredehoek, Cape Town 8001, Western Cape. Tel: +27-21-461-0992.

SHAREWARE/FREEWARE PROGRAMS

Astro-presentation and Astro-analysis, *Digital Coding Methods* (Windows)
www.clmoors.demon.co.uk/

Astrology for Windows, *Halloran Software* (Windows and DOS),
PO Box 75713, Los Angeles, CA 90075, USA.
Internet: www.halloran.com.
US/Canada Toll-Free phone: 1-800-SEA-GOAT (732-4628).
International: (818) 901-1221. Fax: (818) 901-8875.

Astrolog (*Windows, Dos, Mac & Unix*)
Internet: www.magitech.com/~cruiser1/astrolog.htm

RECOMMENDED INTERNET SITES

Matrix Software: http://www.thenewage.com/astrology/astrology.htm

Astrology Newsgroup: alt.astrology (Internet newsgroup, requires newsgroup software)

Astrodienst: http://www.astro.ch
Accurate online horoscope calculation and complete international Time Change Gazetteer (free!).

Metalog Yellow Pages: http://www.astrologer.com
International astrology resource directory, lists schools, astrologers and other resources by country and region.

Astrology World: http://www.astrology-world.com
Traditional techniques, up-to-date news and debate.

Astrology Alive! With Barbara Schermer:
http://www.astrologyalive.com
Experiential astrology.

Astrology.Net: http://astrology.net
Resources, horoscope calculation and range of online interpretations ($).

Edwin Steinbrecher Data Collection: http://www.dome-igm.com
Online celebrity birth data.

The Astrological Association of Great Britain:
http://www.astrologer.com/aanet

The Zodiacal Zephyr: http://www.zodiacal.com/
Astrology resources, some not so serious.

Interconnections: http://www.interconnections.co.uk
Astrology, personality profiling, therapies and more.

Special Offer

Your **Planetary Profile** includes your birthchart in full colour,
together with a full 40–50 page interpretation written by the author,
for only £15.00 (approx. US$24.00) including postage and packing
(usual price £17.50). Send date, time and place of birth together
with cheque (UK) or Visa/Mastercard details to Graham Boston, PO
Box 156, Cheltenham GL52 3YQ (UK). Tel/fax: 01242 228796, or
(+44) 242 228796 from outside the UK.
E-mail gboston@interconnections.co.uk. Laser-printed birthcharts
are also available for £2.50.

APPENDIX 2
RECOMMENDED READING

The following books may be ordered from your local bookstore, or online at **Amazon.com** (http://www.amazon.com)

Astrology, Psychology, and the Four Elements, Stephen Arroyo (CRCS Publications, 1975)

Relationships and Life Cycles, Stephen Arroyo (CRCS Publications, 1975)

Astrology, Karma and Transformation, Stephen Arroyo (CRCS Publications, 1978)

Relating: An Astrological Guide to Living With Others on a Small Planet, Liz Greene (Samuel Weiser, 1979)

Saturn: A New Look at an Old Devil, Liz Greene (Samuel Weiser, 1976)

The Combination of Stellar Influences, Reinhold Ebertin (American Federation of Astrologers, 1972)

Planets in Transit, Robert Hand (Schiffer Publishing Ltd, 1980)

Planets in Composite, Robert Hand (Schiffer Publishing Ltd, 1975)

Planets in Youth, Robert Hand (Schiffer Publishing Ltd, 1977)

Planets in Houses, Robert Pelletier (Schiffer Publishing Ltd, 1978)

Planets in Aspect, Robert Pelletier (Schiffer Publishing Ltd, 1974)

Karmic Astrology: The Moon's Nodes and Reincarnation, Martin Schulman (Samuel Weiser, 1975)

The Eagle and the Lark: A Textbook of Predictive Astrology, Bernadette Brady (Samuel Weiser, 1992)

The Twelve Houses, Howard Sasportas (Thorsons, 1985)

The Round Art, A.T. Mann (WH Smith, 1979)

Mundane Astrology, Michael Baigent, Nicholas Campion, Charles Harvey (HarperCollins, 1984)

Also:

Astrology and Health, Dylan Warren-Davis, Hodder & Stoughton, 1998